FLIGHT AND
METAMORPHOSIS

NELLY SACHS

TRANSLATED FROM THE GERMAN BY

JOSHUA WEINER

WITH

LINDA B. PARSHALL

FLIGHT AND METAMORPHOSIS

POEMS

A BILINGUAL EDITION

FARRAR, STRAUS, AND GIROUX

NEW YORK

Farrar, Straus and Giroux

120 Broadway, New York 10271

"Flucht und Verwandlung," in Nelly Sachs, *Werke*. Kommentierte Ausgabe in vier
Bänden. Herausgegeben von Aris Fioretos, Band 2: *Gedichte 1951–1970*. Herausgegeben
von Ariane Huml und Matthias Weichelt. Copyright © Suhrkamp Verlag Berlin 2010
Translation, Introduction, and Notes copyright © 2022 by Joshua Weiner

Printed in the United States of America
First edition, 2022

Grateful acknowledgment is made for permission to reprint lines
from *Paul Celan: Selections*. Republished with permission of University
of California Press, from *Paul Celan: Selections*, Paul Celan, 2005;
permission conveyed through Copyright Clearance Center, Inc.

Library of Congress Cataloging-in-Publication Data
Names: Sachs, Nelly, author. | Weiner, Joshua, translator. | Parshall, Linda B., translator.
Title: Flight and metamorphosis : poems / Nelly Sachs ; translated by Joshua Weiner
with Linda B. Parshall.
Other titles: Flucht und Verwandlung. English.
Description: Bilingual edition. | New York : Farrar, Straus and Giroux, 2022. | Includes
bibliographical references. | In German and English.
Identifiers: LCCN 2021025270 | ISBN 9780374157081 (hardcover)
Subjects: LCGFT: Poetry.
Classification: LCC PT2637.A4184 F4813 2022 | DDC 831/.914—dc23
LC record available at https://lccn.loc.gov/2021025270

Designed by Crisis

Our books may be purchased in bulk for promotional, educational,
or business use. Please contact your local bookseller or the Macmillan
Corporate and Premium Sales Department at 1-800-221-7945, extension 5442,
or by email at MacmillanSpecialMarkets@macmillan.com.

www.fsgbooks.com
www.twitter.com/fsgbooks
www.facebook.com/fsgbooks

1 3 5 7 9 10 8 6 4 2

CONTENTS

If you had turned on your computer on December 10, 2018, and gone to the Google home page, you would have found the search engine logo adorned with a temporary "doodle," an animated video honoring the birthday not of Emily Dickinson, the American poet we're in the habit of celebrating on that day, but of Nelly Sachs, the Jewish-German (naturalized Swedish) writer who narrowly escaped Nazi Germany in flight with her elderly mother to seek asylum in Stockholm in 1940. (Should you think this a negligible shout-out, keep in mind it was seen over five billion times.) In Berlin that day, you might have opened Google on your phone while watching your kids play in Nelly-Sachs-Park not far from where she was born in Schöneberg; or mailed a letter using a seventy-cent Nelly Sachs first-class stamp; or tuned in to Deutschlandfunk (Germany's NPR), where you might have heard Sachs's poems adapted as lieder and other musical works she inspired by established composers such as Herman D. Koppel, and younger ones, too, like Gerald Eckert; or you could have wandered into Dussmann das KulturKaufhaus, the megamedia store on Friedrichstrasse, to find a shelf of poetry, plays, letters, and miscellaneous prose by Sachs in new and standard editions; or ventured a kilometer farther to Unter den Linden's Pariser Platz and the Akademie der Künste, to pick up a copy of the journal Sinn und Form, which introduced Sachs's Briefe aus der Nacht (Letters from the Night, written around 1950) to the public as recently as 2010.

Sachs has been remembered this way in Germany and largely forgotten in the United States for much the same reason: in both countries, and around the world, Sachs's poetry often plays second fiddle to her role as a cultural symbol. If you're a writer seeking lasting fame, nothing ensures it more than this kind of iconicity; but nothing could be worse if what you want are *readers*. Like any true writer, Sachs wanted readers first, most, and at the end of the day; that she became, after the Second World War, and by virtue of her work, a figure of so-called Jewish reconciliation (with the Germany that murdered six million Jews) was an uncertain fate in the way it framed her writing within the uncontainable horror of the Holocaust. As with reading Anne Frank, reading Sachs, especially if you're Jewish, often takes place at a remove and long before you set eyes on her pages; her name circulates through the collective ethnic consciousness, a kind of glowing word tucked inside other words parleyed between generations. She never quite appears and never disappears; one feels one knows her without ever having taken steps to encounter her where she lives most fully, in her poetry.

This was true for me in October 2015, when I met the poet and translator Alexander Booth at Impala Coffee in Berlin, across the street from Maassenstrasse 12, the birthplace, in 1891, of Leonie (Nelly) Sachs. Alex pointed to the unassuming building marked with a plaque commemorating the spot now housing lawyers' and dentists' offices and a Pilates studio. I almost choked on my coffee. Two years earlier, when I was living in the neighborhood, I had walked past that building many times a day, every day, for a year. I had never noticed. And I had never noticed anyone else noticing either. Alex put in my hand *The Seeker*, a volume of collected poems by Sachs with English translations by Ruth and Matthew Mead and Michael Hamburger, which had been published by Farrar, Straus and Giroux in 1970, the year she died. A gift, he said. I had a feeling I knew why he had presented it to me.

I was back in Berlin that autumn to write about the refugee situation in Germany, to talk with Berliners—Jewish, Christian, Islamic Muslim; native-born and adopted expats; artists, musicians, scholars, religious leaders, citizen volunteers in the ad hoc refugee support network, government workers, shopkeepers; members of the far-right Alternative für Deutschland party and the anti-immigrant Pegida coalition; and refugees from Syria, Iraq, Lebanon, and elsewhere (Germany would take in over 800,000 that year alone). I was learning on the fly about the complexities and commitments, the fears, the resolve, the hopes, ambitions, individual and collective successes and failures; and above all, the living contradictions in play with over a million refugees having entered the country, desperate, exhausted, traumatized by torture and death and endless movement, hungry, angry, solicitous, grateful, accusing—a state of sustained exasperation and despair, at times suppressed, stoically, with wit and the skepticism of the disabused, at other times exposed, appealing, beseeching; at all times (in my experience talking with them) this nightmare, this reality, lived, survived, with dignity and determination.

I opened *The Seeker* and found poems from Sachs's 1959 book, *Flucht und Verwandlung / Flight and Metamorphosis*. Was this not what I was writing about almost sixty years later? Individuals becoming refugees, wandering vast distances, undergoing a social and soulful process of painful change brought about by extreme violence? "O that one understands so little . . ." begins a poem towards the back of the book, and it ends: "Rest / which is only a dead oasis-word—" There is no rest, there can be no rest; for the one in flight, the word signifies an illusion, the yearned-for rest elusive, endlessly deferred, as distant as the dreamed-of return. The poem hit me hard. I looked at the German text of these three lines on the facing page and thought: did the translators get it right? Might a version that sounded better to me also be, in some sense, more in tune with the poem's spirit? Any translation must be an interpretation of the original. What is its authority in relation to the original work? I could hear the accuracy of the translation in front of me, yet . . . *even so*: I felt in the moment that alterations could be made, some small, some larger, which would bring Sachs's poetry—*as I hear it*—into English for the first time. As languages change, as our tongues work words a little differently from one generation to the next, there is always a need to retune, even overhaul, reimagine, and hear again, as if for the first time, an established translation, especially one that's been out of print for many decades. I could sense that the translation had grown stale. Could I do it? With my German? I needed to try.

Versuchen is my favorite word in German, *to try*. Inside the verb one finds another, *suchen*, *to seek*. I looked down again at the title on the cover, *The Seeker*. Nelly Sachs was a poet who believed in signs; what did it mean that I had landed, if only for a short time, in the district that began her journey into what she called "a dustless realm"? How was she speaking *now* to what was happening in Europe and around the world? I was picking up the signal, but the English-language translations by earlier hands often introduced static, a mediating field of a prior era's English that I felt the urge to pass through to reach and somehow hear afresh the poems in German, *Nelly Sachs's German*.

Sachs must have understood something of that desire to hear in her own way the poems she encountered in another tongue, though with a need much more practically pressing, when she landed in Stockholm in 1940, set up with her mother in a tiny flat at Bergsunds Strand 23, and started translating Swedish poetry by members of her generation, such as Pär Lagerkvist and Edith Södergran, and more important yet, younger poets, such as Johannes Edfelt, Harry Martinson, Gunnar Ekelöf, and Erik Lindegren. Seven years later Sachs published *Von Welle und Granit* (From Wave and Granite), a volume of her translations of poems by these and other Swedish writers. This was the first of several anthologies she edited. Although in retrospect she downplayed the importance—outside the little money she made—of translation work in her development as a poet, it was clearly decisive. At forty-nine, her Swedish wasn't fully proficient and never would be. But she was listening intently at the level of syllable and word to a younger generation of poets who, in 1940, had absorbed fifty years of modernist innovation in poetry, much of it Anglophone and American (especially Eliot and Pound), which she would not have had the opportunity to read herself. Her own poetry up till then was still heavily influenced by German Romanticism and the kind of fin de siècle aestheticism associated with the Stefan George circle, shot through with the euphony and rhetoric of a deep inward yearning, often for a lost beloved. For all her modesty, her demure (and perhaps gendered) insistence that she was never a poet, Sachs always exercised the discipline of an authentic artist and later refused, in perpetuity, to allow republication of her work published prior to her flight from Germany (her first book appeared in 1921, when she was thirty years old).

Such refusal was likely due to more than aesthetics. She never reclaimed her German citizenship and returned to Germany only a couple of times in the 1960s, to collect prizes. Her absorption and integration of modernist techniques such as syntactic fragmentation and phrasal juxtaposition, ruptured strophes, elliptical narratives, and other modes of forming, deforming, and re-forming the poetic word happened in conjunction with her learning in 1942 the shocking truth that the Nazi "labor" camps had been, in fact, concentration camps of systematic state-sponsored murder. These mutually involving aspects of art and survival led her to the individuated voice through which she became best known as a poet. "The terrible experiences that have brought me to the brink of death and darkness have been my teachers," she wrote in a letter. "Had I not been able to write, I would not have survived. Death was my teacher. How could I have occupied myself with anything else, my metaphors are my wounds."[1] The great loss of a lover, a member of the resistance who was killed, possibly in front of her; the trauma she experienced during a Nazi interrogation that rendered her mute for days after; the requisition and looting of her family's home; the Nazi "Judaization" of her identity, whereby this secular, assimilated German of Jewish descent was stripped (like all German Jews) of her native nationality by the Nuremberg race laws of 1935; the panic-stricken escape from Berlin (with the help of friends, the intervention of Swedish Nobel laureate Selma Lagerlöf, and even a timely tip received from a sympathetic police officer to avoid the trains)—all these, combined with the desperate circumstances in Stockholm, living with her mother in cramped quarters, translating by day or punching the clock in an archive, and sitting through the night at the small circular kitchen table writing her own poems as her mother's slumbering breath measured the hours when Sachs imaginatively entered the anguished experience of ethnic extinction at the hands of her countrymen. Paradoxically, this long-

---

1. Letter to Gisela Dischner, quoted in her essay "Zu den Gedichten von Nelly Sachs," *Das Buch der Nelly Sachs*, ed. Bengt Holmqvist (Suhrkamp, 1968): 311.

delayed but necessary growth as a poet of distinction found grounding in the sublimation of her self into the collective experience of the Jewish victims of Nazi persecution as it also corresponded to the persecution of Jews throughout history—a devastating rhyme across time. When she gave voice now, in the poems of the early 1940s, what sounded forth, like a racked aria in a nightmare opera of death, was the voice of Jewish suffering.

It's not a welcoming voice but a formidable one; and those poems, collected in the volume In den Wohnungen des Todes (In the Habitations of Death, 1947), remain, for me, very difficult to read— not because of their stylistic or formal strategies, but because she has yet to really travel in her work very far from her poetic origins in the German tradition, despite abandoning conventional meters, stanzas, and rhyming patterns. Here, by way of example, is certainly Sachs's most famous poem, "O die Schornsteine" ("O the chimneys"—it opens the book of 1947, and provides the title for the first volume of English translations published by FSG twenty years later):[2]

O THE CHIMNEYS

And though after my skin worms destroy this
body, yet in my flesh shall I see God. —Job, 19:26

O the chimneys
On the ingeniously devised habitations of death
When Israel's body drifted as smoke
Through the air—

---

2. It should be noted that Sachs's poems in German generally don't have titles, while many English translations have followed the convention of using, as a title, the first line of an untitled poem.

Was welcomed by a star, a chimney sweep,
A star that turned black
Or was it a ray of sun?

O the chimneys!
Freedomway for Jeremiah and Job's dust—
Who devised you and laid stone upon stone
The road for refugees of smoke?

O the habitations of death,
Invitingly appointed
For the host who used to be a guest—
O you fingers
Laying the threshold
Like a knife between life and death—

O you chimneys,
O you fingers
And Israel's body as smoke through the air![3]

As Aris Fioretos, one of Sachs's biographers, points out, if those chimneys strike you as Holocaust kitsch, remember that Sachs is actually introducing a new image into German poetry only a few years after the gas chambers and crematoria were first discovered by Allied troops.[4] One could make the charge of hackneyed imagery about as well as one could accuse Freud of using pop-psychology clichés. No, the problem lies not in the literal object of the chimney

---

3. Translation by Michael Roloff. Nelly Sachs, O the Chimneys (Farrar, Straus and Giroux, 1967): 3. Unless noted, translations in the introduction are mine.

4. Aris Fioretos, Nelly Sachs, Flight and Metamorphosis, trans. Tomas Tranæus (Stanford, 2011): 148.

but maybe in the rhetorical elevation and abstraction—"the ingeniously devised habitations of death" are those ovens (designed by Topf & Söhne, an engineering company, in 1939). But the German word Wohnungen is, in itself, very plain diction—it means simply dwellings, places to live. The word, bold in this context, bites with irony if only Sachs would let it ride and make the connection; instead she breaks the circuit with the full-throated metaphorical phrase striking the tonal high notes, compounded by the repetition of the long lamenting O of invocation; the circular movement of the strophes, which return to their rhetorical starting point; and the linear continuity of the poem's unfolding, which admits no imaginative drift in its voicing, its thinking—all quite conventional, really. Some of these qualities will remain part of her work from here on out; but one finds that the poems become increasingly experimental during the 1950s with her use of radical rupture, symbol-crafting, narrative ellipsis, and other techniques. She will also speak more personally, locating the poems closer to her emotional homespace at the same time as she opens them to a greater range of experience. By virtue of an increasing phrasal compression combined with a broken syntax and a network of mystical metaphors in the later poems, Sachs will create a kind of formal field into which the reader can project herself. (I like Sachs's words durchlöchernd, durchbrochen, meaning perforated or riddled, drilled through with holes—the sense of a tight weave in the fabric of existence opening through material and cosmic processes.) In the earlier poems, to which In den Wohnungen des Todes belongs (many of them chorus cycles in which Sachs speaks with a collective first-person plural voice, a presumptive we), it's as if the reader can do nothing but stand witness to the poem's testimony, as the poem itself stands witness to the atrocity. Such poems come across as imaginatively airtight despite their departure from traditional stanza-making. Sachs's prosopopoeia here admits no process for the reader to experience; form remains static, the discoveries having already been made before the poem begins. However much I try to enter them, such poems from this period, written between 1940 and 1945, stay shut for me; I see them from a distance, or as though displayed behind glass. And these are the poems by Sachs that readers have come to know; provoked by and responding to the Shoah, they claim our attention with a command from outside of us that for me never works its way in.[5] In their iconographic vocal representation of the victims who would otherwise remain silent in their deaths, the poems are beyond reproach—but also beyond reach. These have been the poems reprinted through the decades in anthologies of German poetry, poetry "of witness" and "of survival." They stand, monumental, the poems best known for being known best. Nelly Sachs's reputation was made with them; for them, principally, was she awarded the Nobel Prize in 1966.[6] Well into the twenty-first century Nelly Sachs, dated and tagged, slides all too easily into the textual specimen drawer labeled "Twentieth-Century Genocide: Holocaust." A poet whose mature voice was forged by the Holocaust, she is not a "Holocaust poet" or a "poet of the Holocaust." From this hard-earned but fossilized reputation she should be released.

---

5. *Shoah*, a Hebrew word meaning *total destruction*, has come to refer, in this context, to the Nazis' genocide of European Jews; *Holocaust*, a Greek word meaning *destruction by fire*, refers to the complete catastrophe of the Nazi system of extermination.

6. She shared the prize with the Polish Galician-born writer S. Y. Agnon, who had immigrated to Palestine and helped create modern Hebrew literature.

In flight
what great welcome
along the way—

Shrouded
in the winds' shawl
feet in the sand's prayer
which can never say *Amen*
because it must move
from fin to wing
and further—

The sick butterfly
soon again knows the sea—
This stone
with the fly's inscription
has dropped into my hand—

In place of home
I hold the metamorphoses of the world—

In this, the seventh of fifty-four poems in the sequence that constitutes *Flight and Metamorphosis*, I think we can hear a different set of notes than those struck in the earlier poem "O the chimneys." That poem's passive mode of pathos, of the murdered body rendered into drifting smoke, here finds the living person active, in flight, moving in a constantly evolving state from the earthly elements of sand and water to air and then . . . something else, somewhere else, another dimension. The condition of exile has moved through an imaginative process of transvaluation; the extreme material and psychic difficulties of ongoing migration are part of a world-involving dynamic of metamorphosis, perhaps a dialectic even, in which the homelessness of such transformative stages leads, through a spiritual movement (one completed in the book's final poem), to a longed-for numinous dwelling place. The butterfly, a universal emblem of transformation, is also in Jewish legend a symbol of the soul, but one shared across cultures and ways of valuing—Roman, Aztec, Japanese, Christian—its flight in this poem in apposition to the prehistorical fossil record that links a contemporary political situation of mass migration to an ancient one that the poet holds in her hand as a talisman to carry through an interminable personal exile. There are echoes, as well, with the redemptive flight to freedom, out of enslavement in Egypt, in the fugitive crossing of a sea. (The image of the butterfly occurs in *Flight and Metamorphosis* six times and is a recurring image throughout her work.) The poem's rich complexity opens up even as its cadence quickens, its clipped phrasing and tautened verse line pushing more deeply into the subject. The gross organization *looks* very much the same as that of the earlier work, the poem unfolding in a set of free-verse strophes; but the *internal form* is different: here the reader makes progressive discoveries alongside the poet, the sequence of changes experienced in the shifting figurative movement of the poem itself. As the poem evolves *as a poem*, so too does its perception of evolution as a biological, social, material, and spiritual process. The metamorphoses, though, resist the fanciful; they happen in the world, where actual butterflies migrate thousands of miles, over land and sea, in a journey that takes generations. Emblems of change, of emerging transformation; emblems of migration, of generations of movement over epic distances. Sachs's formal feeling in this poem—the way phrases correspond with the verse line, each line containing a single phrase—reinforces that sense of a dropping verse movement, line to line, with a suddenness that contrasts the dropping stone with the reality of its central emblem, the butterfly, which must continue its forward floating through oceanic space. The poem also recalls the poet's personal experience, not just her own flight as an adult from Germany to Sweden, but the amber fossils she collected along the Baltic as a child, and her fascination with her father's rock collection. (The butterfly, in its sickness, may also be a figure here of the aged and ill and beloved mother; a single symbol can bring together different correspondences.) These correspondences may stay submerged; nonetheless they instill the poem, mysteriously perhaps, with a sense of greater reality. A signature poem, though in a different key than the Holocaust poems, Sachs chose to read it at the Nobel Prize ceremony, in the country that finally welcomed her "along the way."

Flight and Metamorphosis marks the culmination of a period in Sachs's development as a poet. The Shoah, ever present, looms as a shadow in the mind cast over all of Europe; but the living—those who escaped and those who survived—feel close at heart, reachable in a sense through sympathy; and the most recently departed, including her mother in 1950, also haunt her reading of Jewish mystical texts during this period that opened a theological view of the cosmos. That newly framed perception of primary and ultimate matters further changed her writing and broadened the range of feeling for those everywhere caught in a ceaseless migration, a state of never-ending departure. Sachs's poetry of the mid to late 1950s becomes at once more immediately spiritual or, a better word, devotional, and political in a new, more universal way, grounded in the postwar situation, in which up to twenty million people were displaced. And even after 1951, five years after the fighting had ended, a million or more were drifting in search of a place to settle.

As "In flight" suggests, this poetry also attains a lighter body, as if breathing more freely out in the open—a development in her technique in tune with the work's affective change. The expressionist extremity of emotion has shifted into an intuitive, probing, meditative mode that locates the poem's action more convincingly in the psyche of the poet herself. The condition of exile—very much a part of everyday Jewish life in the diaspora and something that connects Jews around the world, however religious or secular, to their biblical ancestors—is no longer defined in her developing vision by an exceptionalism of the divinely chosen, but by a shared political reality: the immediate circumstances of exile and dispersion had become, in her view, general, across the land, shared across time zones and even epochs. For instance, in the ninth poem of the sequence, when we read

Already voiceless—exhaling smoke—

Lying as the sea lies
with just depth below
tearing at the mooring
with waves of longing.

we might readily conjure in our minds the widely published photograph that shook us in September 2015 of the little Syrian boy, Alan Kurdi, drowned off Bodrum in Turkey, in his flight across the sea from the violence of his homeland:

With eyes
turned back toward the motherground—

You, cradled in the century's rut
where time with ruffled wings
drowns, stunned
in the great flood
of your end
without end.

(Is the "You" a lost person; is it the En-Sof, the hidden God?) The difference between speaking *as* and speaking *to* is nuanced, and significant; the shift of the speaker's dramatic position has profound ethical implications. From her modest quarters in Stockholm, where she lives in exile and solitude, Sachs's sympathies lead her to make imaginative contact with "the other" without loss of footing in her own situation, her everyday existence—alone, bereft, surviving in an adopted land and speaking a foreign tongue, where she looks out the kitchen window at night to see the constellations or catch a view of the Hasidic Jews who gather at Sabbath's end to dance and dine in an apartment across the courtyard, "as if in flight."[7]

Flight and Metamorphosis is a book of the night, written with a mind of night that dreams of the sun. Sachs's reading in the *Zohar*, the thirteenth-century "Book of Splendor" or "Radiance," in a translation by the great Jewish scholar Gershom Scholem, and the Hasidic tales and legends collected by Martin Buber, the Jewish theologian, seeded her imagination with a vocabulary for a spiritual exile that fused seamlessly with the elemental conditions of real life on the run. (In fact, the three of them belong to a broad historical milieu of twentieth-century Jewish-German intelligentsia in which they stand as giants of Jewish modernity.) Stars, sand, and sea; dust and thunder; lightning and night skies and travel across the waves; scarves and shrouds—all physical realities for a refugee traveling open distances in search of asylum. The need for rest, the hope of arrival, the wish to be reunited with the beloved—

---

7. Letter to Peter Hamm, Nelly Sachs, *Briefe*, eds. Ruth Dinesen and Helmut Müssener, 4.23.57 (Suhrkamp, 1984): 162.

felt realities that also correspond, in the mythology of the *Zohar*, with a mystical cosmogony in which God, who is everywhere, filling up all space, contracts *into Himself* in order to make room to create the world (a process called *Tsimtsum*), thus in a sense hiding from his own creation in a cosmic withdrawal that leaves us bereft and searching out the mystery of the divine's presence. God, in other words, exists in exile from Himself.[8]

In this cosmogony, the condition of exile is not just historical-political—whether most immediate (the Syrian refugees in Europe now, or the stateless European refugees in Europe after World War II), distant (the expulsion of the Jews from Spain in 1492), or ancient (the Babylonian exile in 586 BC). Since the legend of the expulsion from Eden, the condition of exile in Judaism has been tied to transgression and redemption, to dispersion and homecoming, to enslavement and freedom. (And whether it comes or not, redemption is always already figured theologically into the condition of exile.) With the advent of Kabbalah, the condition of exile figures mystically into God's creative process, in a hidden dimension of reality that also includes language—His creation of the world through the manipulation of cosmic letters read from a primordial Torah that exists outside of time. This kind of transvaluation in the kabbalistic imagination comes charged affectively as

---

8. "According to [Isaac] Luria [Ashkenazi, the sixteenth-century Safed rabbi, one of the originators of Kabbalah], God was compelled to make room for the world by, as it were, abandoning a region within Himself, a kind of mystical primordial space from which He withdrew in order to return to it in the act of creation and revelation." Gershom Scholem, *Major Trends in Jewish Mysticism* (Schocken, 1946; 1954): 260. For consistency, I am using the convention of a male-gendered God as it was used by Sachs, Scholem, Buber, and others.

a great hope (one reason for Kabbalah's popularity in Jewish thought). Thus, the Deus absconditus is very close to us even as He remains veiled beyond our apprehension, our connection to Him primarily a linguistic one: the first acts of creation begin with speech, with our relation to the Thou sustained through the speech of prayer and the reading of the Torah.

Living in isolation; searching for meaning in a world where meaningful structures (social, cultural, and political) appear to have collapsed; desiring connection to something larger than oneself through an enduring fundamental and antecedent relationship— such conditions of Nelly Sachs's existence in Stockholm after the war primed her for the discovery she made in opening the Zohar. If you're a poet, the idea that what you're doing creatively with language, in the invention of a poetic world, constitutes an act of imagination modeled on a divine process, a simulacrum of cosmic origination; that language worked into a higher medium of poetic form can close the distance between oneself and the divine; and even more, that one's poetry participates in a restoration (tikkun olam), across aeons, of an ideal order; that what God conceives, creates, and develops through language could require participation through the devotional work of writing poetry: these powerful ideas figure into a redemptive model of agency the appeal of which to Nelly Sachs, given her circumstances, is easy to imagine.

One aspect of the paradox in Sachs's poetry thus arises; her introduction to the tradition of Kabbalah (of which the Zohar is a part), her involvement with this mystical Jewish work, even from her very limited reading of it, resulted, in the 1950s, in a poetry less defined by the Shoah, an atrocity so momentous it threatened to overshadow all of Jewish experience in the twentieth century, and beyond. In Flight and Metamorphosis, the mystical cosmogonic view of Jewish medieval Spain joins, in spirit, Novalis's metaphysical "blue flower," that unreachable infinite and absolute reality which the German Romantic imagination strove towards, a mysterious path inward, to the deep self, where the budding of mind and world share a single root system. Such living symbols are never pure inventions (*Centaurea cyanus* or cornflower is a common enough flower, after all). Like Novalis, and also Blake and also Rimbaud, Sachs comes into view as a visionary poet who invents her own mythology out of traditional images that have their home in the phenomena of the real, where ideals are always tested in the material processes subject to time.

Hers is not, however, a naturalistically drawn world. We are far, in *Flight and Metamorphosis*, from the "natural supernaturalism" of Romantic poetry; rather we find ourselves in a poetic world where mystical artifice and natural objects join; where biblical prophecy and individual vision fuse; where concrete images transform with surrealistic fluidity; and where abstractions move in colorful animation. "What we are dealing with here," writes Hans Magnus Enzensberger, "are enigmas that do not add up when they are solved, but still retain an enigmatic aspect—and that aspect is what matters."[9] It matters most not because these poems deliver important historical testimonies, but because they initiate the kinds of authentic experiences that happen only in poetry (and that resist critical description).

Whoever's crying
is searching for his melody
which the wind

---

9. Hans Magnus Enzensberger, "Introduction," Sachs, O the Chimneys, 3.

leafed with music
has hidden in night.

Fresh from the source
is too far.

It's time to fly
only with our body.

This associative logic that moves from intuition to intuition in
a kind of dream theorem of the soul; nighttime calculations of sym-
bolic quotients that end with a certain knowledge impossible to
extract from the poem as a linguistic body in flight: to say these
moments take place only in the poem is to miss the force of imag-
ination which understands poetry as the medium that puts us in
a dimension of the real world populated by *facts of a different nature.*
The poems are not just surrealist in style, but intent on modeling
the superreal, the reality of approaching the limit beyond which
one hopes to access a supernal dimension. Such capability may be
a negative one, indeed, and requires from the reader a willingness
not to strain for immediate understanding.

Darkness
widowed
bent over in grief
thunders the long
painful cry of fertility
in ravaged skies

till
the new sunflower
scored by tears
begins to bud
on the morning robe of night—

What does this mean? It means what it says. If you begin by asking in what sense can we understand the *darkness* to be *widowed*, you won't get very far; you have to follow the full sweep of the poet's mind as it moves quickly through a sequence of metaphors: grief brings forth new growth in the heart, just as night and day are mutual preconditions. Okay, very well; that makes sense. But backing up: what is the implication of darkness being widowed? This order of mixed metaphor, Gershom Scholem tells us, is very much a part of the kabbalistic Weltanschauung, a kind of derangement through language that leads to an unworldly perception. "My metaphors are my wounds," Sachs wrote; if she had written instead "My wounds are my metaphors," we'd close the book and move on. The mind of a poet who invents an unforgettable metaphor for her metaphors strikes me as worth following. And one must follow here from poem to poem through the whole sequence; her poetry makes its greatest impact in total, and it works on you *as a book*; the denaturing effect of excerption and isolation in anthologies tends to weaken her poems, which work in concert. Key words (*night, nothing, breath, wind, body, seed, kernel, sand, grain, dust, vein, cord, light, flash, spark, fire, meteor, constellation, refuge, dwelling, possession, longing, rose, blossom, compass, departure, eternity, scream, cry, pain, flight, boundary, land, homeland*) gather force as a reader encounters them in the concatenation of correspondences, poem to poem, each acting as a kind of single point in a great interdependent constellation of sustained symbolic imagination. It has been my task as translator to try to create the combinations of poetic sound and sense that might move the reader's *poetrymind* in concert with such poetry. There's nothing to interpret in any manner that makes rational sense of the whole, as one might do in the reading of a classical allegory, or a modernist one; rather one enters into an experience of signs and ciphers without a preset corresponding code. Like the hidden divine, the meaning of the poem is very close; it lives neither inside nor outside you. This is poetry's irreducible language.

for there's no refuge
to be found
in the flying dust
and only the windscarf
a movable crown
signals, still flickering,
blazoned with restless stars
the course of the world—

"The effect upon the soul of such a work is in the end not at all dependent on its being understood."[10] That's from the introduction of Gershom Scholem's translation of the Zohar, a book in Sachs's possession that she read and annotated, and that would have encouraged her—without much Jewish learning of her own to otherwise draw from—to grow as a poet under the sign of this understanding: that "the secret world of the godhead is a world of language" in which one does "not start from the idea of communicable meaning."[11] Not only are we made in the image of God, but our language too, when it takes the form of poetry, acts as a prime mover. If as the Auden poem declares in his elegy for Yeats, "poetry makes nothing happen" (words that so many who don't seem to like poetry seem to enjoy quoting), one must complete the thought, as

10. Gershom Scholem, ed., Zohar, the Book of Splendor (Schocken, 1949; 1963): ix.

11. Gershom Scholem, On the Kabbalah and Its Symbolism, trans. Ralph Manheim (1960; Schocken, 1965): 36.

Auden does, and acknowledge how "it survives, / A way of happening, a mouth." The event of a poem is a movement of mind that can awaken the conscience, which we could think of as the social action of the soul that puts us and keeps us in relation to others. But there's a whole view of poetry which doesn't predicate that movement on the grasping of paraphrasable content, a view consonant with Kabbalah's emphasis on the pure auditory factor as a function of spiritual transformation. "The symbol 'signifies' nothing and communicates nothing," writes Scholem, "[it] is intuitively understood all at once—or not at all . . . a 'momentary totality' which is perceived intuitively in a mystical now."[12] We are speaking of a now within the realm of unverifiable facts of existence, where poetry is the greater science.

It may seem like I'm trying to have it both ways, a Nelly Sachs who speaks from this book's pages to what we could call the political real, and another Nelly Sachs who tries to realize a deeper relation with the divine through the lightning flash of poetry's pure intuition. Such contradiction is the sine qua non of the visionary poet, whose eyes search the night sky for patterns among the stars and whose hands reveal the hidden roots of the world. The trinity of cosmos, planet, and poem acts as a connecting structure, containing conduits, like "invisible rays," as she wrote to Paul Celan, "that sustain us, through all distances."[13] For the undogmatic Nelly Sachs, this visionary growth of mind flowers in mystic soil; its yearning is for intimacy, direct contact, to find residence within the ultimate enigma, the godhead.

---

12. Scholem, *Major Trends in Jewish Mysticism*, 27.

13. Paul Celan and Nelly Sachs, *Correspondence*, trans. Christopher Clark, ed. Barbara Wiedemann, 9.11.58 (Sheep Meadow, 1995): 11.

But this soil, this earth, is language itself, out of which we grow, material of breath, and the one "dwelling place" all refugees of the current global diaspora carry with them, like the snail Sachs envisions, figured with its "ticking pack of God-time" on its back. This acute sense of loss—of homeland, of family, of tradition and *belonging* in which the flashing tense of *being* joins the extended tension of unceasing *longing* (*Sehnsucht*, a favorite word of Sachs's)—such absence, for the visionary poet, constitutes the very groundwork for the world-making of poetry. In the shifting sands of her creative nightwork, Sachs leaves behind, in these poems of flight and metamorphosis, an exhausted language belonging to an epoch that ended with the Shoah. Other writers in Europe also faced this situation, in which they felt that language and even the conventions of its poetic use had become suspect and degraded as part of a culture that not only allowed the Holocaust to happen but participated in its conception and execution. Sachs never really voiced an opinion in the debates over the literature of "inner emigration" (by writers who held on to the idea of a "real" Germany that literature could help keep alive in the struggle against fascism) and the Trümmerlyrik or "poetry of the rubble" which, in the late 1940s, reflected the physical and moral devastation of the war; yet her later poetry serves as a kind of connector between a dark (*dunkel*) hermeticism and the formally experimental poetry that emerged from a more political postwar attitude towards innovation. While her Nobel Prize fame puts her squarely in the "poetry of the Shoah," where she happened to serve the agendas of reconciliation, her greater oeuvre complicates that picture; reading her poetry book by book, one sees that she doesn't really fit any easy narrative. The epitaphic gestures in some of the poetry, coupled with the olive branch statements she made to Germany in the 1960s, made her a convenient figure for public institutions (especially in West Germany), yet the poems of and around *Flight and Metamorphosis* are more subtle and equivocal in their ambiguities than she was credited for at the time. Sachs is too singular a poet to accommodate generalizations beyond the poems, at once inward turning and outward facing. She may not have been able to resist the attention that came all too easily with the political shift in the West, but her poems resist the broad strokes that sketch that cultural moment. If the prize givers and *Herren Direktoren* of literary institutions willfully read her poems according to their own agendas, Sachs counted on the poets, most of a younger generation, such as Enzensberger and Hilde Domin, to read her with sympathetic insight.

And the friendships Sachs struck up after the war also suggest her desire for fellowship among those younger poets most sensitive to future political tremors along the fault lines of postwar fascist Europe. Of them, none was more important than her friendship with Paul Celan, who wrote to her in May 1958, of "all the unanswerable questions in these dark days." As John Felstiner has suggested, long before they knew each other, Sachs and Celan had in common a traumatized imagination that tapped the same vein of infernal imagery; Sachs's "smoke through the air" (from "O the chimneys") and Celan's "smoke in the air" (from "Todesfuge" / "Death Fugue," his most famous poem, written around the same time) uncannily mirror each other in the immediate post-Shoah moment.[14]

In their friendship, which began in the early 1950s after Celan read some of Sachs's "choral" poems in a journal, they encouraged

---

14. John Felstiner, "Introduction," Celan and Sachs, *Correspondence*, 5.27.58, viii–ix.

each other and considered each other spiritual siblings (though not without tensions). For each of them, this period was one of parallel growth as a poet, although Celan, thirty years younger, and traumatized from his direct experience in the labor camps (where his parents were killed), would go further than Sachs in revolutionizing the German language as a poetic medium. Both poets, however, in their smoke-filled poems of the 1940s, established a subject—genocide in the camps—that they needed to write through. Celan's "Death Fugue," one of the most widely anthologized poems of the Shoah, with its long lines, phrasal repetition, and euphonious cadences, speaks in the collective voice of the murdered Jews, much as Sachs's "O the chimneys" does. Both poems combine, uneasily, the qualities of enchantment and the vocal drama of grief's entrapment. ("Black milk of morning we drink you at dusktime," opens Celan's poem, "we drink you at noontime and dawntime we drink you at night.")[15]

As you can hear, the paradoxical image of Celan's "black milk" echoes the irony of Sachs's "star that turned black" (much like their twinned images of smoke). Likewise, the refinements both would undergo in the development of a late style share remarkably similar traits. In his comparison of "Death Fugue" to Celan's later poems, for example, Pierre Joris charts how Celan's growing concept of fugal form narrows his sense of measure and reference, so that "we no longer know who speaks, who is being addressed; the landscape can be, and is, simultaneously an inner and an outer landscape."[16] As overt reference to the Shoah disappears in Celan's poetry, the language turns more forcefully in on itself, thickening and gaining

15. Paul Celan, "Death Fugue," trans. Jerome Rothenberg, Paul Celan, Selections, ed. Pierre Joris (California, 2005): 46.

16. Pierre Joris, "Introduction," Celan, Selections, 26.

great lexical gravity. With a heightened polysemy that releases multiple meanings, Celan's poems play with and into inherent characteristics of German, the way its semantic roots, made audible at the surface of the language, can be followed into a richly ambiguous linguistic interior, what Celan coined "*Metapherngestöber*," or *metaphor flurries*.[17] "Only one thing remained reachable," writes Celan, "close and secure amid all losses: language . . . But it had to go through its own lack of answers, through terrifying silence, through the thousand darknesses of murderous speech. It went through . . . went through and could resurface, 'enriched' by it all."[18]

In a letter, Sachs writes to Celan, "I, a foreign-language refugee . . . believe in an invisible universe in which we mark out our dark accomplishment. I feel the energy of the light that makes the stone break into music."[19] Sachs's attention to Celan—the way her own poetry prosodically narrowed and drilled down, if not as deeply into German's linguistic root system, then paradoxically in a way that kept her open to possibilities that Celan felt, after the Shoah, were now closed, sealed off—encouraged her at a crucial moment of recasting her poetic craft in response to her reading of Kabbalah. If Sachs called Celan's book *Sprachgitter* (1959) / *Speech-Grille* "Your 'Book of Radiance,' your 'Zohar,'"[20] Celan couldn't follow her into such belief, relating in his poem "Zürich, Zum Storchen" (about their meeting in the Hotel Storchen, in 1960), how they talked

---

17. Pierre Joris, "Introduction," Celan, *Selections*, 27.

18. Paul Celan, *Collected Prose*, trans. Rosmarie Waldrop (Sheep Meadow, 1986): 34.

19. Celan and Sachs, *Correspondence*, 1.9.58, 5.

20. Celan and Sachs, *Correspondence*, 9.3.59, 13.

                           of

the dimming through brightness, of
Jewishness, of
your God.

[. . .]

Of your God was the talk, I spoke
against him[21]

As Celan later wrote, Sachs told him that she was a believer;
Celan responded that he "hoped to be able to blaspheme till the
end."[22] Her reaction, in turn—"It counts Paul it counts / but maybe
otherwise than we think"—he neither accepted nor rejected, but
recorded in the final lines of his poem. Much has been made of
Celan's uneasiness with and criticism of Sachs's striking a repre-
sentative posture of suffering; at the same time, he wrote to her in
affirmation of "the legacy of solitude of which you speak: because
your words exist, it will be inherited, here and there, as the night
is spent. False stars fly over us—certainly; but the grain of dust,
suffused with pain by your voice, describes the infinite path."[23] Re-
ciprocally, Sachs found in Celan's poems, she confided, "a home-
land that I had thought at first would be seized from me by death."[24]
Sachs sometimes despaired, she wrote him, fearing that many
found her poems "not suited for a readership that is looking for
distraction—they are too difficult to understand."[25]

---

21. Translated by Cid Corman, Celan, *Selections*, 76.
22. John Felstiner, "Introduction," Celan and Sachs, *Correspondence*, 5.27.58, x.
23. Celan and Sachs, *Correspondence*, 1958, 7.
24. Celan and Sachs, *Correspondence*, 12.59, 16.
25. Celan and Sachs, *Correspondence*, 5.12.60, 23.

This was an especially hard time for Sachs. The grief after her mother's death in 1950 never having lifted, she continued to live in extreme poverty, and with very little sense of an audience. Psychic frailty would soon give way to psychiatric distress and severe paranoia, and even result in hospitalization. We might think of the poet given to such mystical cast of mind—its association with prophetic statement or vatic sermonizing on the Mount—as working on a stage of broad, if imaginative, presumption and outsize gestures (Whitman and his "barbaric yawp" come to mind); and this is certainly audible in Sachs's Holocaust poems of the 1940s. But the poems of *Flight and Metamorphosis* arise from an abject loneliness, uncertainty, and submissive receptivity that, like the cosmogonic contraction of *Tsimtsum*—God's creative withdrawal from Himself, *into Himself*—suggests a perception predicated on active passivity and searching selflessness. Think of the dreamer, who has relaxed her body and drifted to sleep, a different form of psychic departure.

Night
night
nightdress body
stretching its emptiness
while space expands
from dust without song.

However much we think of poetry as performative, a kind of speech-act—the communication of an understanding that Sachs in her dejection may have felt her poems failed to convey—more fitting yet is the idea of poetry as an art that releases maximum connotation in the language, at the level of the morpheme itself, let alone the word, phrase, sentence, line, strophe. Celan, with his philological learning, intuited the source of this power in a way that helped him develop a new way of writing, a new poetic language; and he did it at a moment when to continue writing any kind of poetry in German required grappling with a reality torn apart by the Shoah. As Sachs's own work developed such a categorical imperative, she found her way forward through poetry's essential element of figuration, a world of ongoing imaginative transformation for which the structured sequence of *Flight and Metamorphosis* unfolds like a verbal map in which one finds one's bearings for a journey into a night of endless stations. Such "metamorphoses of the world" become a kind of dwelling in which her searching for the lost beloved bridegroom, the lost beloved mother, the lost homeland, the distant God, never ceases, never concludes. "Deep dark is always the color of longing for home," she writes in the final poem tracing this meridian of loss, "so night takes me again / into its domain."

That domain, the place of possession, is at once language and beyond language, fearsome in its negative comprehensiveness and also erotically charged, procreative, and made real, if ultimately mysterious, within the final parameters of the field capable of being traced: her poetry. "I wrote them down as the night brought them to me," she wrote, "they came to me as a great secret."[26]

Mystery hides at the heart of this poetry, maybe is the heart of it. In the years I've spent working on this translation, this new *trans/forming* of her work into English, my favorite word of Nelly Sachs's remains impossible for me to capture, unpack, or *activate* properly. The word is *Geheimnis*. Unlike Celan's stunning neolo-

---

26. Letter to Walter Berendsohn, Sachs, *Briefe*, 9.12.44, 41.

gisms, out of which he created a verbal style of multivectored thinking, *Geheimnis* is an ordinary German word, simply meaning *mystery* or *secret*. When Sachs uses *Geheimnis*, she enacts both meanings and more; but in each instance, as translator, I've had to choose one or the other. Sometimes I've opted for *mystery*, as when Sachs writes of "the mystery of affliction" (in the first poem) that manifests as a "branding" of "empyreal skin" and alludes there to a sign of divine marking, a kind of skin-writing (or tattooing, in tense contrast to the Nazi marking of Jewish bodies in the camps), and that signifies God's presence. Other times I've chosen to translate the word as *secret*, such as "the rushing shell of secrets" (in the second poem), where the sound of air in a seashell mimicking surging surf also suggests the sound of the divine presence in creative contraction, like the ebb pulling away from shore. Such secrets and mysteries as belong to esoteric knowledge echo the weirdly blended soundings of Jewish and Christian sources in Sachs, not unlike the kabbalistic works she was reading around this time.

But what's special for Sachs about the word *Geheimnis* lies outside of such traditions; what's uniquely particular, even *particulate*, is the German noun *Heim*, or *home*. Tucked into the mystery, hiding there in plain sight, one finds the source of deepest yearning in the material of language. *Home* / *Heim* is the secret inside the mystery of *Ge/**heim**/nis*, the literal word nesting in the dwelling place of the poem, a mysterious cocoon of language where words contain words like potencies waiting for release, or meanings in hiding. Sachs releases these associations, as *geheim* denotes what's *secret*, or traditionally, in German, *kept at home*, not revealed to strangers. As Ruth Dinesen, another of Sachs's biographers, discovered in the poet's copy of Gershom Scholem's translation of the *Zohar*, Sachs had underlined these words in the book's introduction: *Wort* (word) and *geheime Wirklichkeit* (secret reality). "This is the core of the Zohar," writes Dinesen, "and the core of her own work with poetic expression: the duality of the secret reality of mysticism and the word's unique creative power."[27] Mysticism's root system, tangled in the linguistic derivation of *mystery*, leads to the practice of secret rites, a hidden practice of reading coded revelation; the word also comes from the ancient craft guilds. To practice the mysteries is thus an act of interpretation in reading divine texts in nature, but one that also informs human acts of *poiesis*, of *making*. "To extract / a radium of the word" is how Mina Loy describes Gertrude Stein's method of making something out of words—her poetry, a process that involves intensive and intentional rupture, like Loy's, a release of material deep within language. "Attempt to make materiality transparent through inner languages" is the note Sachs wrote in the margin of her Zohar.[28] "The notion of the poem as epiphany," writes Dinesen—in other words, the poem as *insight*—"connects Nelly Sachs directly to the modern poets of the early twentieth century and assigns her a central position in that period's search for linguistic expression. In her view, mysticism and a modernist conception of language belong inseparably together."[29] The tension between material embodiment (in language) and the self's searching for an absolute reality (outside language) is the hypocenter of modernism's subsurface origination, and a point of multiple intersections. (It connects Sachs to Mallarmé, for example, even as her

---

27. Ruth Dinesen, "The Search for Identity: Nelly Sachs's Jewishness," *Jewish Writers, German Literature*, eds. Timothy Bahti and Marilyn Sibley Fries (Michigan, 1995): 34.

28. Dinesen, *Jewish Writers, German Literature*, 42.

29. Dinesen, *Jewish Writers, German Literature*, 34.

grounding in historical experience also sets her apart.) Modern artists might have pushed hard against the impingement of the real on the ambition of establishing art's autonomous realm, a space akin in some ways to the kind of sacred circle Sachs's poems imagine as a place of refuge, a place for imagination, for realizing possibilities that the material world limits; but they were never able to solve the social and ethical problem of being a body in space and time, in history, in *relation*, as Buber might say. In relation to what? For Sachs, the act of writing, which is the act of *being*, is the act of searching for the answer to that question.

The *Heim* / home that hides at the heart of the mystery, *das Geheimnis*, waits for the seeker, the refugee, and indicates the riddling obscurity that Sachs feared would make her poetry "too difficult." But Sachs's *Tiefdunkel*, her "deep dark," is not a home located outside the self; dwelling, like being, vibrates in language as both noun and verb, an ongoing process of consciousness; one resides in it by virtue of an existential practice that makes it what it is, continually, over and over at every moment. "Deep dark," the color of longing—one finds it in the self, the night domain where one draws closest to God, realized by the desire to be there. The longing is the seeking, is the practice. We could call it *reading*. The journey is interior, the epic search spiritual and condensed in the lyric art at the heart of Nelly Sachs's achievement. The achievement may have been spurred by the Shoah, but Sachs realized it in the forced emigration and sustained exile through which she, like countless others throughout history, at first lost and then continued to feel the loss of home. They were changed, changed utterly, and could never return. Flight and metamorphosis. Nelly Sachs's secret transformations carried her into this mystery of home's location, our situation in the cosmos. In the mysterious practice of translation, English draws close to the spirit of German; we can hear its nearness in a rhyme we won't find in Nelly Sachs's mother tongue. The rhyme between *home* and *poem*.

—J. W.

WASHINGTON, D.C.,

2021

FLIGHT AND
METAMORPHOSIS

WER ZULETZT
hier stirbt
wird das Samenkorn der Sonne
zwischen seinen Lippen tragen
wird die Nacht gewittern
in der Verwesung Todeskampf.

Alle vom Blut
entzündeten Träume
werden im Zickzack-Blitz
aus seinen Schultern fahren
stigmatisieren die himmlische Haut
mit dem Geheimnis der Qual.

Weil Noahs Arche abwärts fuhr
die Sternenbilderstraßen
wird
wer zuletzt hier stirbt
den Schuh mit Wasser angefüllt
am Fuße haben

darin ein Fisch
mit seiner Rückenflosse Heimwehsegel
die schwarz vertropfte Zeit
in ihren Gottesacker zieht.

WHO DIES
here last
will carry the grain of sun
between his lips
will thundercrack the night
in death-throe rot.

Blood-
sparked dreams
will shoot from his shoulders
in a jagged flash
branding empyreal skin
with the mystery of affliction.

Because Noah's ark went down
star-figured avenues
whoever
dies here last
will have shoes
filled with water

where a fish
with homesick backsail
draws black dissolving time
into its tomb.

DIES IST DER DUNKLE ATEM
von Sodom
und die Last
von Ninive
abgelegt
an der offenen Wunde
unserer Tür.

Dies ist die heilige Schrift
in Landsflucht
in den Himmel kletternd
mit allen Buchstaben,
die befiederte Seligkeit
in einer Honigwabe bergend.

Dies ist der schwarze Laokoon
an unser Augenlid geworfen
durchlöchernd Jahrtausende
der verrenkte Schmerzensbaum
sprießend in unserer Pupille.

Dies sind salzerstarrte Finger
tränentropfend im Gebet.

Dies ist Seine Meeresschleppe
zurückgezogen
in die rauschende Kapsel der Geheimnisse.

THIS IS THE DARK BREATH
of Sodom
and the burden
of Nineveh
cast off
at the open wound
of our door.

This the sacred writing
in flight from the land
all its letters climbing
skyward
feathered blessedness
finding refuge in a honeycomb.

This the black Laocoön
cast on our eyelid
perforating millennia
uprooted grieftree
sprouting in our pupil.

These are salt-stiffened fingers
teardropping in prayer.

This His ocean's tow
dragged back
into the rushing shell of secrets.

Dies ist unsere Ebbe
Wehegestirn
aus unserem zerfallenden Sand—

This our ebb
star of agony
from our moldering sand—

WIE LEICHT
wird Erde sein

nur eine Wolke Abendliebe
wenn als Musik erlöst
der Stein in Landsflucht zieht

und Felsen die
als Alp gehockt
auf Menschenbrust
Schwermutgewichte
aus den Adern sprengen.

Wie leicht
wird Erde sein
nur eine Wolke Abendliebe
wenn schwarzgeheizte Rache
vom Todesengel magnetisch
angezogen
an seinem Schneerock
kalt und still verendet.

Wie leicht
wird Erde sein
nur eine Wolke Abendliebe
wenn Sternenhaftes schwand
mit einem Rosenkuß
aus Nichts—

HOW LIGHT
the earth will be
just a cloud of evening's love
when the stone, released as music,
flees the land,

and rocks that squat
like a nightmare
on the human breast
blast the weights of melancholy
from your veins.

How light
the earth will be
yes, a cloud of evening's love
when blackburnt revenge
drawn magnetically
by the Angel of Death
is dead in its snowrobe
silent and cold.

How light
the earth will be
just a cloud, an evening cloud
when star-marks fade
with a rose's kiss
of nothing—

JÄGER
mein Sternbild
zielt
in heimlichen Blutpunkt: Unruhe . . .
und der Schritt asyllos fliegt—

Aber der Wind ist kein Haus
leckt nur wie Tiere
die Wunden am Leib—

Wie nur soll man die Zeit
aus den goldenen Fäden der Sonne ziehen?
Aufwickeln
für den Kokon des Seidenschmetterlings
Nacht?

O Dunkelheit
breite aus deine Gesandtschaft
für einen Wimpernschlag:

Ruhe auf der Flucht.

THE HUNTER
my constellation
takes aim
at a secret bloodpoint: Unrest . . .
and the footstep flees without asylum—

But the wind is no house
just licks the body's wounds
like an animal—

Yet how should we pull time
from the sun's golden threads?
Coil
night
for the silk butterfly's cocoon?

O Darkness
spread your legation wide
for the blink of an eye:

rest on the flight.

SO WEIT INS FREIE GEBETTET
im Schlaf.
Landsflüchtig
mit dem schweren Gepäck der Liebe.

Eine Schmetterlingszone der Träume
wie einen Sonnenschirm
der Wahrheit vorgehalten.

Nacht
Nacht
Schlafgewand Leib
streckt seine Leere
während der Raum davonwächst
vom Staub ohne Gesang.

Meer
mit weissagenden Gischtzungen
rollt
über das Todeslaken
bis Sonne wieder sät
den Strahlenschmerz der Sekunde.

So far out, in the open,
cushioned in sleep.
In flight from the land
with love's heavy luggage.

A butterfly-zone of dreams
like an open parasol
held up against the truth.

Night
night
nightdress body
stretching its emptiness
while space expands
from dust without song.

Sea
with prophetic tongues of spray
rolls
over the death shroud
till sun again sows
each second's blaze of pain.

HEILIGE MINUTE
erfüllt vom Abschied
vom Geliebtesten
Minute
darin das Weltall
seine unlesbaren Wurzeln schlägt
vereint
mit der Vögel blindfliegender Geometrie
der Würmer Pentagramma
die nachtangrabenden

mit dem Widder
der auf seinem Echobild weidet
und der Fische Auferstehung
nach Mittwinter

Einäugig zwinkert
und Herz verbrennend
die Sonne
mit der Löwentatze in der Spindel
zieht sie das Netz um die
Leidenden
dichter und dichter
denn nicht darf man wecken eines
wenn die Seele aushäusig ist

SACRED MINUTE
filled with departing
from the most beloved,
that minute
where the universe
sinks its illegible roots,
united
with the blind-flying geometry of birds
the pentagrammaton of worms
burrowing into night

with the Ram grazing
on the echo of its image
and the resurrection of Pisces
after midwinter.

Blinking, one-eyed
and heart scorching
the sun
with the Lion's paw in the spindle
pulls the net and pulls it
tighter
round those who suffer
—no one may be wakened
when the soul's not home

und seefahrend
vor Sehnsucht
sonst stirbt der Leib
verlassen
in der Winde verlorenem Gesicht.

and seafaring
with longing
else the body dies
cast off
in the lost face of the wind.

IN DER FLUCHT
welch großer Empfang
unterwegs—

Eingehüllt
in der Winde Tuch
Füße im Gebet des Sandes
der niemals Amen sagen kann
denn er muß
von der Flosse in den Flügel
und weiter—

Der kranke Schmetterling
weiß bald wieder vom Meer—
Dieser Stein
mit der Inschrift der Fliege
hat sich mir in die Hand gegeben—

An Stelle von Heimat
halte ich die Verwandlungen der Welt—

IN FLIGHT
what great welcome
along the way—

Shrouded
in the winds' shawl
feet in the sand's prayer
which can never say *Amen*
because it must move
from fin to wing
and further—

The sick butterfly
soon again knows the sea—
This stone
with the fly's inscription
has dropped into my hand—

In place of home
I hold the metamorphoses of the world—

TÄNZERIN
bräutlich
aus Blindenraum
empfängst du
ferner Schöpfungstage
sprießende Sehnsucht—

Mit deines Leibes Musikstraßen
weidest du die Luft ab
dort
wo der Erdball
neuen Eingang sucht
zur Geburt.

Durch
Nachtlava
wie leise sich lösende
Augenlider
blinzelt der Schöpfungsvulkane
Erstlingsschrei.

Im Gezweige deiner Glieder
bauen die Ahnungen
ihre zwitschernden Nester.

DANCER
like a bride
from blind space
you receive
the budding desire
of creation's distant days—

With your body's musical avenues
you graze on the air
there
where the earth
seeks new entry
to birth.

Through
night-lava
like eyelids
softly opening
the first cry
of creation's volcano
flickers.

In the branches of your limbs
the premonitions build
their twittering nests.

Wie eine Melkerin
in der Dämmerung
ziehen deine Fingerspitzen
an den verborgenen Quellen
des Lichtes
bis du durchstochen von der
Marter des Abends
dem Mond deine Augen
zur Nachtwache auslieferst.

Tänzerin
kreißende Wöchnerin
du allein
trägst an verborgener Nabelschnur
an deinem Leib
den Gott vererbten Zwillingsschmuck
von Tod und Geburt.

Like a milkmaid
in twilight
your fingertips tug
the secret sources
of light
till you—pierced by the
trial of evening—
deliver your eyes
to the moon, for the night-watch.

Dancer
twisting in labor
then spent
you alone
bear on your body's hidden cord
the God-given twinned jewels
of death and birth.

KIND

Kind

im Orkan des Abschieds

stoßend mit der Zehen weißflammendem Gischt

gegen den brennenden Horizontenring

suchend den geheimen Ausweg des Todes.

Schon ohne Stimme—ausatmend Rauch—

Liegend wie das Meer

nur mit Tiefe darunter

reißend an der Vertauung

mit den Springwogen der Sehnsucht—

Kind

Kind

mit der Grablegung deines Hauptes

der Träume Samenkapsel

schwer geworden

in endlicher Ergebung

bereit anderes Land zu besäen.

Mit Augen

umgedreht zum Muttergrund—

CHILD
child
in the whirlwind of departure
pushing your toes' white flaming foam
against the burning ring of the horizon
seeking death's secret way out.

Already voiceless—exhaling smoke—

Lying as the sea lies
with just depth below
tearing at the mooring
with waves of longing.

Child
child
your head buried now
the seedpod of your dreams
grown heavy
in final surrender
ready to sow other land.

With eyes
turned back toward the motherground—

Du

in der Kerbe des Jahrhunderts gewiegt

wo Zeit mit gesträubten Flügeln

fassungslos ertrinkt

in der Überschwemmung

deines maßlosen Untergangs.

You,
cradled in the century's rut
where time with ruffled wings
drowns, stunned
in the great flood
of your end
without end.

ZWISCHEN

deinen Augenbrauen

steht deine Herkunft

eine Chiffre

aus der Vergessenheit des Sandes.

Du hast das Meerzeichen

hingebogen

verrenkt

im Schraubstock der Sehnsucht.

Du säst dich mit allen Sekundenkörnern

in das Unerhörte.

Die Auferstehungen

deiner unsichtbaren Frühlinge

sind in Tränen gebadet.

Der Himmel übt an dir

Zerbrechen.

Du bist in der Gnade.

BETWEEN
your eyebrows
is your ancestry
a cipher
out of the sand's oblivion.

You have bent
the sea-glyph
twisted it
in the vise of longing.

You sow yourself with the seeds of every second
into the unheard-of.

The resurrections
of your invisible springtimes
are bathed in tears.

On you, the heavens practice
destruction.

You dwell in grace.

SIEH DOCH

sieh doch

der Mensch bricht aus

mitten auf dem Marktplatz

hörst du seine Pulse schlagen

und die große Stadt

gegürtet um seinen Leib

auf Gummirädern—

denn das Schicksal

hat das Rad der Zeit

vermummt—

hebt sich

an seinen Atemzügen.

Gläserne Auslagen

zerbrochene Rabenaugen

verfunkeln

schwarz flaggen die Schornsteine

das Grab der Luft.

Aber der Mensch

hat Ah gesagt

und steigt

eine grade Kerze

in die Nacht.

JUST LOOK
just look
the human being breaks free
in the middle of the marketplace
do you hear his pulse beating?
And the great city
girds his body
on rubber tires—
because fate
has cloaked
time's wheel—
lifts itself up
on his breath.

Displays behind glass
shattered raven eyes
sparkle out, extinguished,
chimneys shroud in black
the tomb of the air.

But the human being
has said Ah
and ascends
a straight candle
into night.

ABER VIELLEICHT
haben wir
vor Irrtum Rauchende
doch ein wanderndes Weltall geschaffen
mit der Sprache des Atems?

Immer wieder die Fanfare
des Anfangs geblasen
das Sandkorn in Windeseile geprägt
bevor es wieder Licht ward
über der Geburtenknospe
des Embryos?

Und sind immer wieder
eingekreist
in deinen Bezirken
auch wenn wir nicht der Nacht gedenken
und der Tiefe des Meeres
mit Zähnen abbeißen
der Worte Sterngeäder.

Und bestellen doch deinen Acker
hinter dem Rücken des Todes.

BUT MAYBE
in a smokecloud of error
we have
created a wandering cosmos
with the language of our breath—

Have we
time and again
sounded the fanfare
of the beginning
shaped the grain of sand
quick as wind
before, once more, there was light
above the bud of the embryo?

And again
we are encircled
in your districts, and again,
though we don't recall the night
nor the depths of the sea
with our teeth we bite off
the star-veins of words.

And still we work your field
behind death's back.

Vielleicht sind die Umwege des Sündenfalles
wie der Meteore heimliche Fahnenfluchten
doch im Alphabet der Gewitter
eingezeichnet neben den Regenbögen—

Wer weiß auch
die Grade des Fruchtbarmachens
und wie die Saaten gebogen werden
aus fortgezehrten Erdreichen
für die saugenden Münder
des Lichts.

Maybe the detours of man's fall
are like the secret desertions of meteors
marked in the alphabet of storms
alongside rainbows—

And who knows
the course of becoming fertile
how seeds bend up
out of depleted soil
for the suckling mouths
of light.

Im Alter

der Leib wird umwickelt
mit Blindenbinden
bis er kreist
hilflos
in Sonnenfinsternis.

Aber tief
im Meeresgang
Unruhe hebt
und senkt sich
in den gekreuzten Flügeln.

Tod
kaum gereift
ist schon neu befruchtet
aus Gräbern
das Öl der Heiligkeit gezogen.

Gestirne
in der Auferstehung
brennen Dunkelheit an.

Wieder ist Gott reisefertig.

IN OLD AGE
the body is wrapped
with blindfolds
till it spins
helplessly
in the solar eclipse.

But deep
in the sea's coursing
unrest rises
and sinks
in the crossed wings.

Death
barely ripened
is already reseeded
the sacred oil
drawn up from graves.

In the resurrection
stars
scorch the darkness.

And again, God is ready to depart.

UNEINNEHMBAR
ist eure nur aus Segen errichtete
Festung
ihr Toten.

Nicht mit meinem Munde
der
Erde
Sonne
Frühling
Schweigen
auf der Zunge wachsen läßt
weiß ich das Licht
eures entschwundenen Alphabetes
zu entzünden.

Auch nicht
mit meinen Augen
darin Schöpfung einzieht
wie Schnittblumen
die von magischer Wurzel
alle Weissagung vergaßen.

So muß ich denn aufstehen
und diesen Felsen durchschmerzen
bis ich Staubgeworfene

IMPREGNABLE
is your fortress
(you, the dead)
built only of blessings.

Not with my mouth—
which allows
Earth
Sun
Spring
Silence
to grow on the tongue—
do I know how to light
the lamp of your vanished
alphabet—

And not
with my eyes
where creation migrates
like cut flowers
that have forgotten
every prophecy of their magic roots.

So I must rise up
and suffer this rock
till covered in dust

bräutlich Verschleierte
den Seeleneingang fand
wo das immer knospende Samenkorn
die erste Wunde
ins Geheimnis schlägt.

veiled like a bride
I find the soul's gate
where the budding seed
inflicts the first wound
on the mystery.

DAVID

erwählt

noch in der Sünde

wie Springflut tanzend

gebogen

in heimlichen Mondphasen

vor der Bundeslade

losgerissene Erdwurzel

Heimwehgischt.

Aber

im Flammentopf der Erde

mit Pflanze und Getier

die Lenden hinauf

standen noch die Propheten

sahen aber schon

durch Gestein

hin zu Gott.

Christus nahm ab

an Feuer

Erde

Wasser

baute aus Luft

noch einen Schrei

DAVID
chosen
still in sin
like springtide dancing
curving
in secret moonphases
before the Ark of the Covenant
earth-roots ripped out
homesick spindrift.

But
still standing in the flamepot of the earth
with plants and animals
up to the loins
the prophets were
already looking
through stone
to God.

Christ gave up
fire
earth
water
yet built one more cry
out of air

und das
Licht
im schwarzumrätselten Laub
der einsamsten Stunde
wurde ein Auge
und sah.

and the
light
within the leaves' dark enigma
of the most solitary hour
became an eye
and saw.

EINER
wird den Ball
aus der Hand der furchtbar
Spielenden nehmen.

Sterne
haben ihr eigenes Feuergesetz
und ihre Fruchtbarkeit
ist das Licht
und Schnitter und Ernteleute
sind nicht von hier.

Weit draußen
sind ihre Speicher gelagert
auch Stroh
hat einen Augenblick Leuchtkraft
bemalt Einsamkeit.

Einer wird kommen
und ihnen das Grün der Frühlingsknospe
an den Gebetmantel nähen
und als Zeichen gesetzt
an die Stirn des Jahrhunderts
die Seidenlocke des Kindes.

SOMEONE
will snatch the ball
from the hands
of those who can hardly play.

Stars
have their own laws of fire
and their fertility
is the light,
and reapers and gleaners
are not from here.

Their storehouses
are far away
even straw
in a flash of luminous power
paints solitude.

Someone will come
and sew the springbud's green
onto their prayer shawl
and as a sign
on the century's brow
the silken locks of the child.

Hier ist

Amen zu sagen

diese Krönung der Worte die

ins Verborgene zieht

und

Frieden

du großes Augenlid

das alle Unruhe verschließt

mit deinem himmlischen Wimpernkranz

Du leiseste aller Geburten.

Here is the time
to say *Amen*
this coronation of words
moving into hiding
and
peace
you, great eyelid,
which shuts out all unrest
with your celestial wreath of lashes

You, gentlest of all births.

MISCHUNG

dieser Mutter

dieses Vaters

unterm geschlossenen Augenlid

aus Stern.

Wo wärest du

wo wäre ich

wo unsere Liebe versteckt

wenn anders verschlungen

der Kometenschweife Umarmung

himmlisches Begräbnis

in Sonnenfinsternis

die Sekunde vertrauert

oder

der Mond mit zaubernder Weißhand

pulsende Meeresader

rückwärts gezügelt

in Ebbe und Tod—

Einmal verschlossen

in der Geburtenbüchse der Verheißungen

seit Adam

die Frage schläft zugedeckt

mit unserem Blut.

THE MIXING OF
this mother
this father
beneath the closed
star-spun lid.

Where would you be
where would I be
where would our love be hidden
if otherwise entangled
the comet tail's embrace
skybound burial
in a solar eclipse
the second mourned
or
the moon with conjuring white-hand
pulsing sea-vein
reined backwards
in ebb and death—

Once sealed up
in the birth-box of promises
ever since Adam
the question has been sleeping
covered in our blood.

GERETTET

fällt vieles

in die Körbe der Erinnerungen

denn

auch dieses Nachtalter

wird seine Fossile haben

die schwarz geränderten Trauerschriften

seines schief gewachsenen Staubes.

Vielleicht

auch werden unsere nachgelassenen

Himmel

diese blaßblauen Steine

heilende Magie üben

in andere Höllen niedergelegt

wird

dein Sterbegespräch

im Wehe-Wind

dem kalten Gespann der

sich streckenden Glieder

Zeiten durchatmen

und

glasbläserhaft biegen

verschwundene Liebesform

für den Mund eines Gottes—

SAVED,
many things fall
into the baskets of memories
because
even this age of night
will have its fossils
the black-bordered elegies
of its crookedly piled dust.

Maybe too
the heavens
we've left behind
these pale blue stones
set down in other hells
will practice healing magic

and your dying words
will
in the griefwind
in the cold yoke
of stretching limbs
breathe for aeons
and
like glassblown shapes
bend the vanished form of love

for the mouth of a god—

So ist's gesagt—
mit Schlangenlinien aufgezeichnet

Absturz.

Die Sonne
chinesisch Mandala
heilig verzogener Schmuck
zurück in innere Phasen heimgekehrt
starres Lächeln
fortgebetet
Lichtdrachen
zeitanspeiend
Schildträger war die Fallfrucht Erde
einst
goldangegleist—

Weissagungen
mit Flammenfingern zeigen:
Dies ist der Stern
geschält bis auf den Tod—

Dies ist des Apfels Kerngehäuse
in Sonnenfinsternis gesät

so fallen wir
so fallen wir.

So it's said—
drawn in snaking lines

plunge.

The sun
Chinese mandala
divinely warped jewel
turned in inward phases
back home twisting,
smile fixed
in constant prayer
light-dragon
spitting at time
the shield bearer was earth's wind-fallen fruit
once
scorching-bright gold—

Prophecies
point with flaming fingers:
This is the star
husked to death—

This is the apple's core
sown in the solar eclipse

so we fall
so we fall.

Vertriebene
aus Wohnungen
Windgepeitschte
mit der Sterbeader hinter dem Ohr
die Sonne erschlagend—

Aus verlorenen Sitten geworfen
dem Gang der Gewässer folgend
dem weinenden Geländer des Todes
halten oft noch in der Höhle
des Mundes
ein Wort versteckt
aus Angst vor Dieben

sagen: Rosmarin
und kauen eine Wurzel
aus dem Acker gezogen
oder
schmecken nächtelang: Abschied
sagen:
Die Zeit ist um
wenn eine neue Wunde aufbrach
im Fuß.

Reißend wird ihr Leib
im Salz der Marter fortgefressen.

THOSE DRIVEN
from home
wind-whipped
with the death-vein behind the ear
slaughtering the sun—

Cast off from lost customs
following the watercourse
and the weeping rails of death
they still hold
in the cave
of the mouth
a word hidden
for fear of thieves

they say: rosemary
and chew a root
pulled from the field
or
taste night after night: departure
they say:
Time is over
as a new wound opened
on the foot.

Their body soon devoured
by the salt of torment.

Hautlos
augenlos
hat Hiob Gott gebildet.

Skinless
eyeless
did Job form God.

KLEINER FRIEDEN
in der durchsichtigen Stunde
am Levkojengrab
im Abendrot trompetet Jenseits.

Gloriole des Palmenblattes
Wüstenoffenbarung der Einsamkeit.

Der Ahne Leben
im leuchtenden Andachtsbuch
ruhend auf Murmelbaches Schlummerrolle
und Muschel an das Ohr gelegt
mit Spieluhrmelodie.

O großer Ozean im kleinen Ohr!
O Menuett der Liebe
oblatenzartes Stundenbuch

auch das war Leben—
der gleiche Schlaf in schwarz Magie
und Dorn der die vergessene Rose
des Blutes
in Erinnerung sticht

A MOMENT OF PEACE
in the transparent hour
at the gillyflowered grave—
the next world trumpets in the red of sunset.

Gloriole of the palm leaf
desert revelation of solitude.

The ancestor's life
in the glowing book of devotions
resting on the murmuring brook's soft bolster
and shell held to the ear
with its music-box melody.

O deep wide ocean in the little ear!
O minuet of love
waferlight book of hours

that too was life—
the same black magic sleep
and thorn that engraves
the forgotten rose
of blood
onto memory

gezähnter Blitz
in des Gewitters Maskentanz
verdunkelnd
auch diese Elfenbeinküste.

toothed lightning
in the thunderstorm's masked dance
darkening,
too, this ivory coast.

HIER IST KEIN BLEIBEN LÄNGER
denn aus seinem Grunde spricht schon Meer
die Brust der Nacht
hebt atmend hoch
die Wand, daran ein Kopf
mit schwerer Traumgeburt gelehnt.

In diesem Baustoff
war kein Sternenfinger
mit im Spiel
seit das Gemisch im Sand begann
so lebend noch im Tod.

Wer weint
der sucht nach seiner Melodie
die hat der Wind
musikbelaubt
in Nacht versteckt.

Frisch von der Quelle
ist zu weit entfernt.

Zeit ists zu fliegen
nur mit unserem Leib.

HERE THERE'S NO STAYING LONGER
for the sea already speaks from its depths
the breast of night, breathing,
lifts the wall high
on which a head leans
in heavy dreambirth.

Ever since the stirring began in the sand
no star-finger
played a part
in this mortar we build with
so even in death they're alive.

Whoever's crying
is searching for his melody
which the wind
leafed with music
has hidden in night.

Fresh from the source
is too far.

It's time to fly
only with our body.

MUTTER

Meerzeitgeblüh

nächtlicher Ort

für der Ozeane Arom

und die Niederkunft

des erleuchteten Sandes—

Umzogen von göttlicher Ellipse

mit den beiden Schwellenbränden

Eingang

und

Ausgang.

Dein Atemzug holt Zeiten heim

Bausteine für Herzkammern

und das himmlische Echo der Augen.

Der Mond hat sein Schicksal

in deine Erwartung gesenkt.

Leise vollendet sich

die schlafende Sprache

von Wasser und Wind

im Raum deines

lerchenhaften Aufschreis.

MOTHER
bloom of sea-time
night place
for the oceans' aroma
and the birth
of glowing sand—

By divine ellipse
compassed
with both thresholds burning
entry
and
exit.

Your breath brings home times past
building blocks for heart chambers
and the eyes' heavenly echo.

The moon has sunk
its destiny into your expectation.

The sleeping speech
of water and wind
quietly culminates

in the space of your
lark-like cry.

UND ÜBERALL
der Mensch in der Sonne
den schwarzen Aderlaß Schuld
werfend in den Sand—
und nur im Schlaf
dem tränenlosen Versteck
mit dem lodernden Pfeil des Heimwehs
fahrend aus dem Köcher der Haut—

Aber hier
immer nur Buchstaben
die ritzen das Auge
sind aber lange schon
unnütze Weisheitszähne geworden
Reste eines entschlummerten Zeitalters.

Jetzt aber
der Wettercherub
knotet
das Vier-Winde-Tuch
nicht um Erdbeeren zu sammeln
in den Wäldern der Sprache
sondern
die Trompete veränderlich anzublasen
im Dunkel

AND EVERYWHERE
the human in the sun
throwing the black bloodletting, *guilt*
onto the sand—
and only in sleep
the hiding place with no tears
with the blazing arrow of homesickness
flying from the skin's quiver—

Here, though,
just letters
that scratch the eye
but already long ago became
useless wisdom teeth,
remains of an age gone numb.

But now
the weather-cherub
ties
the four-winds scarf
not to pick strawberries
in the forests of speech
but rather
to blow the trumpet one way, then another
in the darkness

denn nicht kann Sicherheit sein
im fliegenden Staub
und nur das Kopftuch aus Wind
eine bewegliche Krone
zeigt noch züngelnd
mit Unruhgestirnen geschmückt
den Lauf der Welt an—

for there's no refuge
to be found
in the flying dust
and only the windscarf
a movable crown
signals, still flickering,
blazoned with restless stars
the course of the world—

LANGE
sichelte Jakob
mit seines Armes Segen
die Ähren der Jahrtausende
die in Todesschlaf hängenden
nieder—
sah
mit Blindenaugen—
hielt Sonnen und Sterne
einen Lichtblick umarmt—
bis es endlich hüpfte
wie Geburt aus seiner Hand
und
in Rembrandts Augenhimmel hinein.

Joseph
schnell noch
versuchte den Blitz
des falschen Segens
abzuleiten
der aber brannte schon
Gott-wo-anders auf—

Und der Erstegeborene losch
wie Asche—

FOR A LONG TIME
Jacob
with the blessing of his arm
scythed down
the grain of millennia
hanging in the sleep of the dead—
saw
with blind eyes—
held suns and stars
in his arms
for a bright blissful moment—
till finally all leapt
like birth from his hand
and
into Rembrandt's celestial eye.

Joseph
still tried
quickly
to deflect
the flash of false blessing
already flaring up
God-knows-where—

And the firstborn went out
like embers—

Selbst die Steine umarmen wir—
wir haben einen Pakt mit ihnen geschlossen—
HIOB

HALLELUJA
bei der Geburt eines Felsens—

Milde Stimme aus Meer
fließende Arme
auf und ab
halten Himmel und Grab—

Und dann:
Fanfare
in der Corona des Salzes
ozeangeliebtes
wanderndes Zeitalter
stößt granitgehörnt
in seinen Morgen—

Halleluja
im Quarz und Glimmerstein

beflügelte Sehnsucht
hat ihren Schlüssel himmelwärts gedreht

We embrace even the stones—
with them, we have made a pact—

JOB

HALLELUJAH
at the birth of a rock—

Mellow voice of the sea
flowing arms
up and down
hold heaven and grave—

And then:
fanfare
in the corona of salt
ocean-beloved
wandering epoch
pushes granite-horned
into its morning—

Hallelujah
in the quartz and glimmering stone

winged desire
has turned its key heavenwards

Tief-Nacht-Geburt
aber schon Heimat für eines Seevogels
Ruhesturz
Feuerflüchtlinge
aus blinden Verstecken entflohen
ausgewinterte Chemie
in geheimer Unterhaltung des Aufbruchs—

Sonnensamen
aus geöffneten Mündern der Offenbarung

Halleluja
der Steine im Licht—

Versiegelte Sterngewänder
durchbrochen
und der Himmel mit der ziehenden Sprache
öffnet Augen an umweinter Nacktheit—

Aber
im Mutterwasser
saugende Algen umklammern
den füßehebenden Dunkelleib
Fische in Hochzeitskammern
wo Sintflut bettet
reigen besessen

gefolterte Träume gerinnen
in der Meduse atmend Saphirgeblüh

deep-night-birth
yet home already for a seabird's
soft plunge
refugees of fire
fled from blind hiding places
winter-killed chemistry
in secret talk of departure—

sun-seeds
from opened mouths of revelation

Hallelujah
of the stones in the light—

Sealed-up star-garments
perforated
and the heavens, with drifting speech
open eyes on lamented nakedness—

But
in the motherwater
sucking algae clasp
the footlifting darkbody,
fish, obsessed, dance round
in wedding chambers
where the flood is bedded down

tortured dreams congeal
in the sapphire-blossom that breathes the medusa

und wie mit Wegweisern zeigend
Blutkorallen aus schläfrigem Tod—

Halleluja
bei der Geburt eines Felsens

in die goldene Weide des Lichts—

and blood corals
like signposts
show the way
out of drowsy death—

Hallelujah
at the birth of a rock

into the golden pasture of light—

SCHON
reden knisternde farbige
Bänder
fremde Münder
neue Heiligensprache.

Schon
rollen unter den Flügeln der Adler
die Sterbelaken der Horizonte fort
denn auch des Todes Drama
schmerzt seine Zeitläufte ab
weiß
hinter dem Vorhang
um neuen Beginn.

Hier aber
mit gekrönten Haaren
die Herrscher zwischen Sternenhaufen
im Ei der Nacht
verspielen mit gesetzten Tafeln
weissagende Fernen
in die drehenden Scheiben der Windrose.
Besprechen Wunden mit Salz
bis Luft weinend nach Hause zieht
Musiktüren schließend.

Already
crackling, colored
ribbons are speaking
strange mouths
new language of saints.

Already
the horizons' death shrouds
unwind under the eagles' wings
because even the drama of death
survives its painful timecourse
knows
a new beginning
behind the curtain.

But here
with crowned locks
the sovereigns, between star-clusters
in the egg of night
and with tables set
gamble away prophetic distances
into the spinning disks of the compass rose.
They cast spells
heal wounds with salt
till the air goes home weeping
pulling closed the music-doors.

Dunkelheit
verwitwet
schmerzgekrümmt
gewittert der Fruchtbarkeit
langen Klageruf
in brandgeschatzte Himmel

bis
die neue Sonnenblume
tränengeätzt
den Trauermantel der Nacht
anzuknospen beginnt—

Darkness
widowed
bent over in grief
thunders the long
painful cry of fertility
in ravaged skies

till
the new sunflower
scored by tears
begins to bud
on the morning robe of night—

SCHLAF WEBT DAS ATEMNETZ
heilige Schrift
aber niemand ist hier lesekundig
außer den Liebenden
die flüchten hinaus
durch die singend kreisenden
Kerker der Nächte
traumgebunden die Gebirge
der Toten
übersteigend

um dann nur noch
in Geburt zu baden
ihrer eigenen
hervorgetöpferten Sonne—

SLEEP WEAVES THE BREATHNET
holy scripture
but no one here can read
except for the lovers
fleeing
out through the singing circling
dungeons of the nights,
dreambound, rising over
the mountains
of the dead

only then
to bathe in the birth
of their own
hand-thrown sun—

Es springt
dieses Jahrhundert
aus seinem abgeschuppten Todkalender—

Es pfeift um das Haar der Berenice
ein Peitschenblitz—

Es hat sich Adams Haupt geöffnet
empor steigt zuckend
in den dünnen Strich der Luft:

Die sieben Tage Schöpfung.

Es sprießt ein Samenkorn in Angst
schnell auf einem Menschenfinger.
Der Adler trägt im Schnabel seinen Kinderhorst.

Einen Kuß gab noch der Bienensaug der Mädchenlippe
dann sichelt der Tod das Windgetreide.

Entgleiste Sterne werden nachtschwarz angestrichen
erlöst sprühen die fünf Sinne wie Leuchtraketen auf—

Und Schweigen ist ein neues Land—

THIS CENTURY
springs
out of its molted calendar of death—

A whip's flash whistles
round starlit Berenice's Hair—

Adam's head has opened
rises flickering
into the thin streak of air:

The seven days of creation.

In fear, a seed sprouts
quick on a human finger.
In his beak, the eagle carries his children's aerie.

The white nettle kissed the girl's lip
before death scythed the wind's harvest.

Derailed stars are painted nightblack,
released, the five senses spark like flares—

And silence is a new land—

WIE VIELE

ertrunkene Zeiten

im rauschenden Schlepptau des Kinderschlafes

steigen ein auf hoher See

in die duftende Kajüte

spielend auf mondenen Gebeinen der Toten

wenn die Jungfrau mit der nachtgesprenkelten

Sonnenlimone

hineinblendet

aus Schiffsuntergang.

Hilflos

auf und zu

schlagen der Augenblicke Schmetterlingstüren

unverschließbar

für die goldenen Lanzen

die mordbrennenden

in das blutende Schlachtfeld der Kinderangst.

Was für Umwege sind zu gehen

für Herzschritte

bevor endlich

das Erinnerungsboot

das tagfahrende

erreicht ist—

HOW MANY
drowned epochs,
in the rushing wake of childhood sleep
on the high seas,
enter the fragrant cabin,
play on the moon-white bones of the dead
when Virgo, with the nightspeckled
sun-lemon,
dazzles down
from the sinking ship.

Helplessly
swinging open and closed
the butterfly-doors of these moments
cannot be sealed shut
against the golden lances,
murderburning,
into the bleeding battlefield of childhood fright.

What detours still lie ahead
for heart-steps
before
the memory boat
traveling by day
is finally reached—

Wie viele traumumspülte Grenzen der Erde
sind auszuziehen
bis Musik kommt
von einem fremden Gestirn—

Wie viele todkranke Eroberungen
müssen sie machen
ehe sie heimkehren
Mondmilch im Munde
in die schreiende Luft
ihrer hellbewimpelten Kinderspielplätze—

How many dreamlapped borders of the earth
are yet to be traced
till music comes
from a strange star—

How many conquests
must they make, sick unto death,
before they return home
moonmilk in the mouth
into the clamoring air
of their brightly bannered playgrounds—

KOMMT EINER
von ferne
mit einer Sprache
die vielleicht die Laute
verschließt
mit dem Wiehern der Stute
oder
dem Piepen
junger Schwarzamseln
oder
auch wie eine knirschende Säge
die alle Nähe zerschneidet—

Kommt einer
von ferne
mit Bewegungen des Hundes
oder
vielleicht der Ratte
und es ist Winter
so kleide ihn warm
kann auch sein
er hat Feuer unter den Sohlen
(vielleicht ritt er
auf einem Meteor)
so schilt ihn nicht
falls dein Teppich durchlöchert schreit—

IF SOMEONE COMES
from afar
with a language
that maybe seals off
its sounds
with a mare's whinny
or
the chirping
of young blackbirds
or
like a gnashing saw that severs
everything in reach—

If someone comes
from afar
moving like a dog
or
maybe a rat
and it's winter
dress him warmly
for who knows
his feet may be on fire
(perhaps he rode in
on a meteor)
so don't scold him
if your rug, riddled with holes,
screams—

Ein Fremder hat immer
seine Heimat im Arm
wie eine Waise
für die er vielleicht nichts
als ein Grab sucht.

A stranger always has
his homeland in his arms
like an orphan
for whom he may be seeking nothing
but a grave.

WEITER
weiter
durch das Rauchbild
abgebrannter Liebesmeilen
hin zum Meer
das grollend beißt
seinen Horizontenring in Stücke—

Weiter
weiter
hin zum Schwarzgespann
mit dem Sonnenkopf im Wagen
das auf weiße Mauern steigt
durch den Stacheldraht der Zeit
in das Auge des Gefangenen sinkt
blutbeträuft—
bis der endlich
weiter
weiter
mit dem Schlaf verbrüdert
in die große Freiheit läuft—

Schon hat ihn der Traum gefangen
in dem sterngeschlossenen Zirkel . . .

FURTHER
further
through the smoking vision
of scorched miles of love
leading down to the sea
growling, chewing up
the ring of its horizon—

Further
further
down to the black team of horses
with the sun's head in the chariot
that mounts the white walls
through the barbed wire of time
and sinks into the prisoner's eye
wet with blood—
until finally
further
further
with sleep as his brother
he runs into the great freedom—

Already the dream has caught him
in the star-closed circle . . .

OHNE KOMPASS
Taumelkelch im Meer
und
die Windrose des Blutes tanzend
im Streit mit allen Himmelslichtern
so der Jüngling—

Versucht seine Jugend
mit dem Gegenwind im Haar
weiß noch nichts von der Vorsicht
des Schattens in blendender Sonne.

Auf seinem Lärmgott
durchschneidet er
des sinkenden Abends flehende Hände
und pfeift die Bettelei des Alters
in den Wind.

Die Nacht
entgürtet er der Sterne
wirft
diese abgedufteten Lavendellieder
der Urmutter
zwischen die Leinewand.

Doch steigt er gerne die Treppe
zum Himmel hinauf

WITH NO COMPASS
the cup of trembling in the sea
and
the dancing windrose of the blood
at odds with all the lights of heaven
thus, the young man—

Tests his youth
with the headwind in his hair
knowing nothing yet of the shadow's wariness
in the dazzling sun.

On his god of noise
he cuts through
the sinking evening's pleading hands
and whistles into the wind
the beseeching of old age.

From the night
he unbinds the stars
throws between the folds
these tired lavender lullabies
of the great mother
their fragrance long lost.

Yet how glad to climb the stairs
up to the sky

die Aussicht zu erweitern
denn er ist gespannt von Tod
wie ein Blitz
ohne Wiederkehr.

Von den Schaukelstühlen
heimisch gewordener Geschlechter
stößt er sich ab

außer sich geraten
mit dem Feuerhelm
verwundet er die Nacht.

Aber
einmal fällt Stille ein
diese Insel
gelagert schon
an letzter Atemspitze des Lebens
und
aus zeitverfallendem Stern
tönt Musik
nicht fürs Ohr—

Er aber
hört das Samenkorn flüstern

im Tod—

to expand the view
since he's supercharged by death
like a lightning bolt
that only strikes once.

From the rocking chairs
of complacent generations past
he pushes himself off

distraught
he wounds the night
with the helmet of fire.

But one day
silence will fall—
this island
already attached
to the last sharp gasp of life—
and
from a dying star
music will sound
not for the ear—

But he
hears the seed whispering

in death—

WEIT FORT
von den Kirchhöfen
weine ich um dich
aber auch nicht in die Lüfte
und nicht in das wartende Meer.

Weit fort
von allen längst verschmerzten
Zeitaltern
in Mumiensteinen
eingesargten—

Nur in die Sehnsucht
das wachsende Element
lege ich meine Träne—

Hier ist außerhalb und innen.

Diese Lichterpyramide
ausgemessen in anderen Räumen
mit Begrabenen von allen Königreichen
bis ans Ende der Trauer—

Mit den Altären der Seele
die ihr Sakrament
lange schon hinter dem Augenlid
verbargen—

FAR AWAY
from the churchyards
I cry for you
but not into the air
and not into the waiting sea.

Far away
from those times
long past and forgotten
interred
in the mummy tombs of stone—

I let my tears fall
only into longing
the swelling element—

Here is both outside and in.

This pyramid of lights
measured in other spaces
with buried bodies from every kingdom
till the end of mourning—

With the altars of the soul
which have long hidden
their sacrament
behind the eyelid—

WO NUR SOLLEN WIR HINTER DEN NEBELN
die Wurzel der Hauche suchen
die in den Wolken Augenblicks-Schöpfungsgeschichte schreiben?
Was zieht da ein in den windigen Leib
für mutterloses Gesicht?
Welche Ader zersprang um der heiligen Geometrie der Sehnsucht
in deinen Augen Heimat zu geben?

Mit Wasserblumen
weinend ausgeziert
fliegt die Waise im hellgrünen Gras
erfundene Umarmung
lange vor des Menschen Eintritt
in den Lehm.

Das Neue ist Gottes—
Seine Erstlinge dort oben winken
Verwandtschaft.
Eva umschlängelt
spielt Erdapfelspiel.

Einmal beschworen
der Stier stößt gesichelt durch Zeiten
sein Bild gewebt in hautloser Glorie—

Yet where in the mists
shall we seek the roots of those breaths
writing this moment's history of creation
in the clouds?
What kind of motherless face
moves into the airy body?
Which vein burst
to offer the holy geometry of yearning
a homeland in your eyes?

Decorated with waterflowers
weeping
the orphan flies in bright green grass
imagined caress
long before man enters
into the clay.

All that's new belongs to God—
His firstborn up there signal
kinship.
Eve ensnaked
plays the earth's apple game.

Once evoked
Taurus, scythe-cut, pushes through the epochs
his image woven in skinless glory—

Geistesgestört flattert Prophetenbart
abgerissen von der Botschaft der Lippe
Moment des wandernden Schrittes
und der Gebärde des Tragens
ehe sie in die Schwergewichte der Menschengeburt fielen
im Schrei—

Deranged, the prophet's beard flutters
torn from the lip's message
moment of the wandering footstep
and the gesture of bearing
before they plunged into the labored
weight
of human *being*
screaming—

LINIE WIE
lebendiges Haar
gezogen
todnachtgedunkelt
von dir
zu mir.

Gegängelt
außerhalb
bin ich hinübergeneigt
durstend
das Ende der Fernen zu küssen.

Der Abend
wirft das Sprungbrett
der Nacht über das Rot
verlängert deine Landzunge
und ich setze meinen Fuß zagend
auf die zitternde Saite
des schon begonnenen Todes

Aber so ist die Liebe—

LINE LIKE
living hair
drawn
deathnight-darkened
from you
to me.

Bridled
on the outside
I am bowed down
thirsting to kiss
the end of distances.

The evening
is throwing the springboard
of night over the crimson
lengthening your headland
and I place my foot, hesitating,
on the quivering string
of death, already begun

But such is love—

DER SCHLAFWANDLER

kreisend auf seinem Stern

an der weißen Feder des Morgens

erwacht—

der Blutfleck darauf erinnerte ihn—

läßt den Mond

erschrocken fallen—

die Schneebeere zerbricht

am schwarzen Achat der Nacht—

traumbesudelt—

Kein reines Weiß auf Erden—

THE SLEEPWALKER
circling on his star
awakens
to the dawn's white feather—
the bloodstain there reminding him—
he lets the moon
drop, appalled—
the snowberry bursts
on the night's black agate—
dreamstained—

No pure white on earth—

WEISSE SCHLANGE

Polarkreis

Flügel im Granit

rosa Wehmut im Eisblock

Sperrzonen um das Geheimnis

Herzklopfenmeilen aus Entfernung

Windketten hängend am Heimweh

flammende Granate aus Zorn—

Und die Schnecke

mit dem tickenden Gepäck der Gottzeit.

WHITE SERPENT
polar circle
wings in granite
pink sorrow in the iceblock
forbidden zones around the mystery
heartpounding miles from distance
wind chains hanging on homesickness
flaming shell of fury—

And the snail
with the ticking pack of God-time.

WELCHE FINSTERNISSE
hinterm Augenlid
angeglänzt
von der explodierenden Abendsonne
des Heimwehs

Strandgut
mit dem Seezeichen
königlich
schlafbewachsen

Schiffbruch
Hände aus den Wellen
fliehende Versuche
Gott zu fangen

Bußweg
umarmend
Meilensteine aus Meer

O keine Ankunft
ohne Tod—

WHAT ECLIPSING DARKNESS
behind the eyelid
lit up
by the evening's exploding sun
of homesickness

jetsam
with the seamark
royally
overgrown with sleep

shipwreck
hands reaching out of the waves
fleeting attempts
to capture God

path of penitence
embracing
milestones from the sea

O no arrival
without death—

WENN DER ATEM
die Hütte der Nacht errichtet hat
und ausgeht
seinen wehenden Himmelsort zu suchen

und der Leib
der blutende Weinberg
die Fässer der Stille angefüllt hat
die Augen übergegangen sind
in das sehende Licht

wenn ein jedes sich in sein Geheimnis
verflüchtigte
und alles doppelt getan ist—
Geburt
alle Jakobsleitern der Todesorgeln hinaufsingt

dann
zündet ein schönes Wettergeleucht
die Zeit an—

WHEN THE BREATH
has built the hut of night
and goes out
to seek its drifting place in the heavens

and the body
the bleeding vineyard
has filled the casks of silence
the eyes have passed over
into the seeing light

when every last one
has vanished into its mystery
and everything is done twice—
birth
sings its way up every Jacob's ladder of death's pipe organs

then
a lovely lightning flash
ignites time—

WIE VIELE HEIMATLÄNDER
spielen Karten in den Lüften
wenn der Flüchtling durchs Geheimnis geht

wie viel schlafende Musik
im Gehölz der Zweige
wo der Wind einsam
den Geburtenhelfer spielt.

Blitzgeöffnet
sät
Buchstaben-Springwurzelwald
in verschlingende Empfängnis
Gottes erstes Wort.

Schicksal zuckt
in den blutbefahrenen Meridianen einer Hand—

Alles endlos ist
und an Strahlen
einer Ferne aufgehängt—

HOW MANY HOMELANDS
play cards in the air
as the refugee passes through the mystery

How much sleeping music
in the wooded thicket
where the wind, all alone,
plays the midwife.

Lightning-split
the alphabet-spurgewood
sows
in devouring conception
God's first word.

Fate twitches
in the bloodcoursing meridians of a hand—

Everything is endless
and hung on the rays
of a distance.

ENDE
aber nur in einem Zimmer—
denn
über die Schulter mir schaut
nicht dein Gesicht
aber
wohnhaft in Luft
und Nichts
Maske aus Jenseits

und Anruf
Hof nur aus Segen herum
und nicht zu nah
an brennbarer Wirklichkeit

und Anruf wieder
und ich gefaltet eng und kriechend
in Verpuppung zurück
ohne Flügelzucken
und werde fein gesiebt
eine Braut
in den durstenden Sand—

AN END
but only in a room—
for
what's looking over my shoulder
is not your face
but
residing in air
and nothing—
mask from beyond

and a calling
around me
a halo only of blessings
and never too close
to reality
so ready to burn

and again a calling
and I, folded tight and crawling
back into the cocoon
without a wing's flicker
I will be a bride
finely sifted
into the thirsting sand—

TOD

Meergesang
spülend um meinen Leib
salzige Traube
durstlockende in meinem Mund—

Aufschlägst du die Saiten meiner Adern
bis sie singend springen
knospend aus den Wunden
die Musik meiner Liebe zu spielen—

Deine entfächerten Horizonte
mit der Zackenkrone aus Sterben
schon um den Hals gelegt
das Ritual des Aufbruchs
mit dem gurgelnden Laut der Atemzüge
begonnen
verließest du nach Verführerart
vor der Hochzeit das bezauberte Opfer
entkleidet schon fast bis auf den Sand
verstoßen
aus zwei Königreichen
nur noch Seufzer
zwischen Nacht und Nacht—

DEATH
song of the sea
sweeping round my body
salty grape
making my mouth thirsty—

If you strike the strings of my veins
till they jump singing
budding from the wounds
to play the music of my love—

Your fanned-out horizons
with the jagged crown of dying
already laid round the neck
the ritual of departure
with breath's gurgling noise
begun—
if you left like a rakehell before the wedding
the enchanted victim
already stripped almost to sand
cast out
from two kingdoms
nothing but sighs
between night and night—

SCHON
mit der Mähne des Haares
Fernen entzündend
schon
mit den ausgesetzten
den Fingerspitzen
den Zehen
im Offenen pirschenden
das Weite suchend—

Der Ozeane Salzruf
an der Uferlinie des Leibes

Gräber
verstoßen in Vergessenheit
wenn auch Heilkraut für Atemwunden—

An unseren Hautgrenzen
tastend die Toten
im Schauer der Geburten
Auferstehung feiernd

Wortlos gerufen
schifft sich Göttliches ein—

Already
with the mane of hair
lighting up distances
already
with the exposed
fingertips
toes
stalking in the open
searching the vastness—

The salt-call of the oceans
at the shoreline of the body

Graves
cast out into oblivion
even if healing herbs for breathwounds—

At the borders of our skin
the dead, groping
in the shudder of births
celebrating resurrection

Wordlessly summoned
the divine embarks—

INMITTEN
der Leidensstation
besessen von einem Lächeln
gibst du Antwort
denen
die im Schatten fragen
mit dem Mund voll gottverzogener Worte
aufgehämmert
aus der Vorzeit der Schmerzen.

Die Liebe hat kein Sterbehemd mehr an
versponnen der Raum
im Faden deiner Sehnsucht.
Gestirne prallen rückwärts ab
von deinen Augen
diesem
leise verkohlenden Sonnenstoff

aber über deinem Haupte
der Meeresstern der Gewißheit
mit den Pfeilen der Auferstehung
leuchtet rubinrot—

DEEP INSIDE
the station of suffering
possessed by a smile
you answer
those
who question in the shadows
their mouths full of god-deformed words
hammered out
from pain's distant past.

Love no longer wears a shroud,
space is spun
in the thread of your longing.
Stars ricochet
back from your eyes
sunsubstance
softly turning to char

but over your head
Stella Maris, lodestar of certainty,
glows ruby red
with the arrows of resurrection—

ACH DASS MAN SO WENIG BEGREIFT
solange die Augen nur Abend wissen.
Fenster und Türen öffnen sich wie entgleist
vor dem Aufbruchbereiten.

Unruhe flammt
Verstecke für Falter
die Heimat zu beten beginnen.

Bis endlich dein Herz
die schreckliche Angelwunde
in ihre Heilung gerissen wurde
Himmel und Erde
als Asche sich küßten in deinem Blick—

O Seele—verzeih
daß ich zurück dich führen gewollt
an so viele Herde der Ruhe

Ruhe
die doch nur ein totes Oasenwort ist—

O THAT ONE UNDERSTANDS SO LITTLE
as long as the eyes know only evening.
Windows and doors open as if knocked off track
before you ready for departure.

Unrest inflames
hiding places for night moths
beginning to pray for home.

Until at length your heart
dreadful hooked wound
was torn into healing,
heaven and earth
as cinders kissing in your gaze—

O Soul—forgive
my wanting to lead you back
to so many hearths of rest

Rest
which is only a dead oasis-word—

HINTER DEN LIPPEN
Unsagbares wartet
reißt an den Nabelsträngen
der Worte

Märtyrersterben der Buchstaben
in der Urne des Mundes
geistige Himmelfahrt
aus schneidendem Schmerz—

Aber der Atem der inneren Rede
durch die Klagemauer der Luft
haucht geheimnisentbundene Beichte
sinkt ins Asyl
der Weltenwunde
noch im Untergang
Gott abgelauscht—

BEHIND THE LIPS
the unutterable waits
tears at the umbilical cords
of words

the martyr's death of the alphabet
in the mouth's urn
spiritual ascension
out of searing pain—

But the breath of inner speech
through the wailing wall of air
whispers a confession freed of secrets,
sinks into the asylum
of the world's wound
even in its downfall
still overheard by God—

ALLE LANDMESSENDEN FINGER
erheben sich
von den Staubgrenzen
und
augenbesät
das Tuch der Cherubim um die Schläfen
so sieht der Blick
durch entleerte Linse der Sonne.

Schlaf überfällt Dächer und Wände.

Auch der Engel hat Abschied genommen
bekränzt mit Traum.

Rauschend am Gehör vorbei
das Floß
beseelt mit dir

Wir sind
nur wir

ALL FINGERS SURVEYING THE LAND
rise up
from the borders of dust
and
eye-sown
the scarf of cherubim round the temples
thus the gaze sees
through the empty lens of the sun.

Sleep assails roofs and walls.

Even the angel has taken leave
garlanded with dream.

A rushing sweep past the ear
the raft
inspirited by you

We are
just us

ANGEÄNGSTIGT
mit dem Einhorn Schmerz durchstochen—

Wächter
Wächter
ist die Nacht schon um?

O du Drama schwarze Zeit
mit unendlichem Gerede
hinter dornverschlossenem Mund.

Blitze
salzversteinert wetzen
Reue die im Blut begraben—

Wächter
Wächter
sage deinem Herrn:
Es ist durchlitten—

und
Zeit den Scheiterhaufen
anzuzünden
der Morgen singt
und nachtgeronnen Blut
im Hahnenschrei
soll fließen—

FRIGHTENED
by the unicorn's piercing pain—

Watchman
watchman
is the night already over?

O you drama, black time
with endless talk
behind a thorn-stitched mouth.

Thunderbolts
salt-petrified
whet repentance buried in blood—

Watchman
watchman
tell your Lord:
it has been endured—

and
time to light
the pyre
the morning sings
and night-curdled blood
in the cock's cry
must flow forth—

ABGEWANDT
warte ich auf dich
weit fort von den Lebenden weilst du
oder nahe.

Abgewandt
warte ich auf dich
denn nicht dürfen Freigelassene
mit Schlingen der Sehnsucht
eingefangen werden
noch gekrönt
mit der Krone aus Planetenstaub—

die Liebe ist eine Sandpflanze
die im Feuer dient
und nicht verzehrt wird—

Abgewandt
wartet sie auf dich—

TURNED AWAY
I wait for you
who linger, far from the living
or near.

Turned away
I wait for you
since those who've been freed
cannot be captured
by coils of longing
or crowned
with the crown of planetary dust—

love is a plant in desert sands
it serves in fire
and is not consumed—

Turned away
it waits for you—

EINE GARBE BLITZE

fremde Macht

besetzen

diesen Acker aus Papier

Worte lodern

tödliches Begreifen

Donner schlägt das Haus ein

darin Grablegung geschah.

Nach Vergebung dieses Lebens

aus verzehrter Schreibeweise

aus der einzigsten Sekunde

hebt der innere Ozean

seine weiße Schweigekrone

in die Seligkeit zu dir—

A LIGHTNING SHEAF
alien power
takes over
this field of paper
words flaring
deadly understanding
thunder destroys the house
where burial took place.

After forgiveness of this life
out of such writing, consumed
exhausted, *spent*—
out of the singular second
the inner ocean lifts
its white crown of silence
in blissfulness, to you—

UND IMMER
die Wahrsager des Himmels
hinter angelehnten Türen
oder
sternenrückwärts gewachsen
wie Spiegelschrift—

Und die salzigen Flügel
duftend vom Meer
abgelegt an der Schwelle
und Fischernetze
immer zum Trocknen aufgehängt—

Und die blitzweißen Adern der Erleuchtung
längst in Daniels Träume eingegangen—

Fächelt etwas
wie Wind am Haar unserer Unwissenheit?

Löffelt Tod den Stein
fort bis in den Staub?

Meer
hingekniet singt Prophetia
in gemuscheltes Ohr

AND ALWAYS
the prophesiers of heaven
behind doors left ajar
or
grown, in stellar reversal,
like mirror-writing—

And the briny wings
smelling of the sea
laid on the doorstep
and fishing nets
hung up to dry—

And the searing white veins of enlightenment
received long ago in Daniel's dreams—

Is something, like the wind,
fanning the hair of our ignorance?

Is death spooning away the stone
until it is dust?

Sea
kneeling, sings prophecies
into the scalloped ear

vorausgesagte Sterngeometrie
in der Honigwabe
damit Sonne süß werde?

Zyklen der Liebe wachsend
transparent wie Kristall
über Schlafgrenzen hinaus?

Asche
nur Verband für den Schmerz des Lichtes
auf Erden?

star-geometry
foretold in the honeycomb
so the sun may become sweet?

Cycles of love expanding
clear as crystal
beyond the borders of sleep?

Ashes
just a dressing for the pain
of light on earth?

ERLÖSTE

aus Schlaf

werden die großen Dunkelheiten

der Steinkohlenwälder

auffahren

abwerfen

das glitzernde Laub

der Lichterjahre

und ihre Seele aufdecken—

Beter

nackend

aus Blitzen

und Gesang aus Feuer

kniend

stoßend

mit Geweihen des Außer-sich-Seins

wieder an den Klippen des Anfangs

bei der Wogenmütter

Welt einrollender Musik.

Released
from sleep
the great darknesses
of coal forests
will rise
throw off
the glittering foliage
of years of lights
and uncover their soul—

Supplicant
naked
from lightning
and song of fire
kneeling
thrusting again
with antlers of fury,
beside your self at the cliffs of the beginning,
in the world-enfolding music
of the mothers
of the waves.

SO RANN ICH AUS DEM WORT:

Ein Stück der Nacht
mit Armen ausgebreitet
nur eine Waage
Fluchten abzuwiegen
diese Sternenzeit
versenkt in Staub
mit den gesetzten Spuren.

Jetzt ist es spät.
Das Leichte geht aus mir
und auch das Schwere
die Schultern fahren schon
wie Wolken fort
Arme und Hände
ohne Traggebärde.

Tiefdunkel ist des Heimwehs Farbe immer

so nimmt die Nacht
mich wieder Besitz.

SO I POURED FORTH FROM THE WORD:

a piece of night
with arms outstretched
just a set of scales
to weigh the fleeing
this star-time
sunk in dust
with the tracks set down.

Now it is late.
The lightness is leaving me
and also the heaviness
my shoulders are already moving on
like clouds
arms and hands
without any gesture of bearing.

Deep dark is always the color of longing for home

so night takes me again
into its domain.

NOTES ON THE
TRANSLATION AND SOURCES

A FURTHER NOTE ON THE TRANSLATION

It's often possible to translate a poem from one language into another as a *prose paraphrase* and give some basic sense of the poem's meaning. But a *poetic* translation of a poem, qua poem, is an act of re-creation. In the case of Nelly Sachs, it requires attention to at least two immediate linguistic levels, because standard German and Nelly Sachs's German are not quite the same thing. My attempt has been to create an experience in English analogous to reading her German; linguistic equivalence remains a metaphor, a holy grail. Still, regarding her language and her form, which is to say her *poetry*, I have put a premium on the values that Elizabeth Bishop once expressed about her own poetry: *accuracy, spontaneity, mystery*. I have aimed to maintain Sachs's free-verse lineation, keeping to her pattern of isolating certain words on a line; her strophic structure; her style of apposition, which tends to float phrases in grammatical ambiguity; her rhythmic tension; her expressionist and irreal imagery (often captured in neologism and compound substantives, which the German language encourages and accommodates); her tonal levels, from elevated to more earthy; and the manner in which words and phrases repeat from poem to poem—part of the fundament of coherence in a visionary work that contains levels of rich if obscure evocation.

The German of Nelly Sachs is strange. One could even say, going further, that her poems are strangers to German, even that they remain strangers in Germany, as estranged as they are currently championed there. The irony of this predicament is not only literary; the political circumstances of the poems' composition keep them in exile, just as Nelly Sachs herself was kept, by an emotionally internalized political situation, from ever resettling in her homeland.

While it may be true that, like all native speakers of English, I will continue to learn English throughout my life, sometimes actively, more often (at this point, in my late fifties) passively, I am an active student of German language and literature. But this is a relatively new pursuit for me, and whatever fluency I may have in poetry generally, my limitations in German are immediately obvious to anyone who knows the language. Still, I wanted to try my hand at translating Nelly Sachs, while at the same time making sure that I didn't make mistakes having to do with technical aspects of the language beyond my ken. For this, I needed help, and was lucky to get it in the friendship and tutelage of Linda B. Parshall, professor emerita of German language and literature at Portland State University and a literary translator with roots in medieval scholarship. (If you're interested in language and you have the chance to work with a medievalist, *do it*.)

I made all initial drafts of Sachs's poems into English, which I then brought to Linda, who reviewed the drafts with me against Sachs's German line by line, strophe by strophe. At other times, Linda caught errors and arrived at solutions on her own, researched literary enigmas with great resource and indefatigable scholarly ardor, and showed me where in the text I had stumbled. We worked together this way for a couple of years. Her devotion to helping with this impossible work was an inspiration when the inspiration of Sachs's poems themselves sometimes left me deflated with their difficulty. The German of Nelly Sachs is such that some questions of grammar, in the process of translating, raised issues of style, which required, in turn, degrees of interpretation that I could not manage on my own. Linda's deep knowledge of German language, literature, and culture—from the Middle Ages to the present day—informs this translation. In some areas—such as works of Jewish mysticism, the postwar political situation in Germany, and the range of Sachs scholarship in both English and (to some degree) German—I brought many months of reading and research to bear on contextual understanding, the life story, and the interpretation of difficult individual passages. In addition, I have sometimes ignored Linda's good advice about phrasing in order to stay true to my own way of hearing Sachs's poems, and thus may have introduced errors for which she is not responsible; at other times, her authoritative technical good sense and sensitivity to Sachs's poetics won the day and saved me embarrassment. In the end, I made all final decisions about the translation; any errors in the text are mine.

There are some minor spelling discrepancies between the first two German editions of 1959 and 1968, such as ist's versus ists; my translation follows the standard text established by the Suhrkamp edition of 2010.

English translations of some of Nelly Sachs's poetry were collected in two volumes from Farrar, Straus and Giroux (now long out of print): O the Chimneys: Selected Poems, Including the Verse Play, Eli (1967) and The Seeker, and Other Poems (1970). The translators of the first volume (1967) are Michael Hamburger, Ruth and Matthew Mead, Michael Roloff, and Christopher Holme (who translated the play); of the second (1970), Ruth and Matthew Mead and Michael Hamburger. Each volume contains selections from the oeuvre organized chronologically by book. Translations of the sixteen poems from Flight and Metamorphosis included in the 1967 volume are distributed among the three principal translators of the lyric poetry; Ruth and Matthew Mead are credited for the thirty-four poems in the 1970 volume. There has been no published translation of Flucht und Verwandlung in its entirety; the current book is the first appearance of Flight and Metamorphosis, complete, in English.

Other English translations of Nelly Sachs currently in print include an edition of the late sequence Glühende Rätsel (1964) / Glowing Enigmas translated by Michael Hamburger (Tavern Books, 2013), which collects in one volume those translations dispersed in the Farrar, Straus and Giroux volumes of 1967 and 1970; six poems translated by Eavan Boland, collected in her anthology After Every War: Twentieth-Century Women Poets (Princeton, 2004); and the correspondence between Nelly Sachs and Paul Celan, translated by Christopher Clark, edited by Barbara Wiedemann, and with an introduction by John Felstiner (Sheep Meadow, 1995). Miscellaneous poems from 1967 and 1970 are included in anthologies such as *Against Forgetting: Twentieth-Century Poetry of Witness*, edited by Carolyn Forché (Norton, 1993); *Twentieth-Century German Poetry*, edited by Michael Hofmann (Farrar, Straus and Giroux, 2006); and *Michael Hamburger: A Reader*, edited by Dennis O'Driscoll (Carcanet, 2017). Some (rogue) translations unauthorized by the literary estate have appeared here and there in small journals and on the web, and can be found by those seekers so inclined.

OTHER BOOKS

I've learned much about the life and work of Nelly Sachs from Aris Fioretos's "illustrated biography," *Nelly Sachs, Flight and Metamorphosis*, translated by Tomas Tranæus (Suhrkamp, 2010; Stanford, 2011). Some scholarly monographs have also been helpful, most notably Ursula Rudnick's *Post-Shoa Religious Metaphors: The Image of God in the Poetry of Nelly Sachs* (Peter Lang, 1995); Kathrin M. Bower's *Ethics and Remembrance in the Poetry of Nelly Sachs and Rose Ausländer* (Camden House, 2000); Elaine Martin's *Nelly Sachs: The Poetics of Silence and the Limits of Representation* (De Gruyter, 2011); and Jennifer M. Hoyer's *"The Space of Words": Exile and Diaspora in the Works of Nelly Sachs* (Camden House, 2014). Some individual pieces that were helpful include Ehrhard Bahr's "Flight and Metamorphosis: Nelly Sachs as a Poet of Exile," from *Exile: The Writer's Experience*, edited by John M. Spalek and Robert F. Bell (Chapel Hill, 1982); Ruth Dinesen's essay "At Home in Exile: Nelly Sachs: Flight and Metamorphosis," in *Facing Fascism and Confronting the Past: German Women Writers from Weimar to the Present*, edited by Elke P. Frederiksen and Martha Kaarsberg Wallach (SUNY, 2000); and Jean Boase-Beier's essay "Translating the Poetry of Nelly Sachs," in *The Palgrave Handbook of Literary Translation* (2018). I also benefited from reading *Jewish Writers, German Literature: The Uneasy Examples of Nelly Sachs and Walter Benjamin*, edited by Timothy

Bahti and Marilyn Sibley Fries (Michigan, 1995); Andrew Shanks's chapter "'After Auschwitz': The Case of Nelly Sachs," in *What Is Truth: Towards a Theological Poetics* (Routledge, 2001); and Katja Garloff's chapter "Nelly Sachs and the Myth of the 'German-Jewish Symbiosis,'" in *Words from Abroad: Trauma and Displacement in Postwar German Jewish Writers* (Wayne State, 2005). I also consulted *Das Buch der Nelly Sachs*, edited by Bengt Holmqvist (Suhrkamp, 1968) and *Briefe der Nelly Sachs*, edited by Ruth Dinesen and Helmut Müssener (Suhrkamp, 1984).

About Kabbalah, and most specifically the *Zohar*, I tried to follow the trail of Nelly Sachs's own reading, and therefore paid greatest attention to Gershom Scholem's edition, *Zohar, the Book of Splendor: Basic Readings from the Kabbalah* (Schocken, 1949; 1977); *Major Trends in Jewish Mysticism* (Schocken, 1946; 1954); and *On the Kabbalah and Its Symbolism* (Schocken, 1960; 1965). But I also learned from Daniel C. Matt's translation, *Zohar: The Book of Enlightenment* (Paulist Press, 1983), and his anthology, *The Essential Kabbalah: The Heart of Jewish Mysticism* (HarperCollins, 1995). Peter Cole's anthology (especially his introduction and notes) *The Poetry of Kabbalah: Mystical Verse from the Jewish Tradition* (Yale, 2012) was a great resource of instruction and pleasure; and Harold Bloom's essay on that particular work, collected in *Possessed by Memory: The Inward Light of Criticism* (Knopf, 2019), illuminated further.

Likewise, about Hasidism, and other strains of Jewish-German thinking, I followed Nelly Sachs's lead into Martin Buber's *I and Thou*, translated by Ronald Gregor Smith (1923; Scribner's, 1958); *Tales of the Hasidim: Early Masters* (Schocken 1947; 1970) and *Later Masters* (Schocken, 1948), both translated by Olga Marx; *Ten Rungs: Hasidic Sayings* (Schocken, 1947; 1962), translated by Olga Marx; *The Way of Man* (1948; Routledge, 1994); *Two Types of Faith*, translated by Norman P. Goldhawk (Macmillan, 1951); *The Legend of the Baal-Shem*, translated by Maurice Friedman (1955; Princeton, 1995); *Hasidism and Modern Man*, edited and translated by Maurice Friedman (Harper & Row, 1958); and also *The Way of Response*, edited by N. N. Glatzer (Schocken, 1966). Other pertinent theological works I made use of include Simone Weil's *Gravity and*

Grace, translated by Emma Crawford and Mario von der Ruhr (1947; Routledge, 1999), and Abraham Joshua Heschel's *God in Search of Man* (Farrar, Straus and Giroux, 1955; 1977).

About German literature, I continue to learn from Michael Hamburger's example as poet, translator, and critic, especially, in this case, his classic *Reason and Energy: Studies in German Literature* (Routledge, 1957); *The Truth of Poetry: Tensions in Modern Poetry from Baudelaire to the 1960s* (Methuen, 1969; 1982); and *After the Second Flood: Essays on Post-war German Literature* (St. Martin's, 1986).

Other miscellaneous works that I found useful include George Steiner's *Language and Silence* (Atheneum, 1967); Susan Gubar's *Poetry after Auschwitz: Remembering What One Never Knew* (Indiana, 2003); *A New History of German Literature*, edited by David E. Wellbery and Judith Ryan (Harvard, 2004); Hannah Arendt's *The Jewish Writings*, edited by Jerome Kohn and Ron H. Feldman (Schocken, 2007); Judith Ryan's *Introduction to German Poetry* (Cambridge, 2012); and *Makers of Jewish Modernity*, edited by Jacques Picard et al. (Princeton, 2016).

We seem to be enjoying a boom in critical writing about translation. I found most useful Rainer Schulte and John Biguenet's anthology *The Craft of Translation* (Chicago, 1989), and the companion volume of classic essays, *Theories of Translation: An Anthology of Essays from Dryden to Derrida* (Chicago, 1992). Also of select interest were essays from *In Translation: Translators on Their Work and What It Means*, edited by Esther Allen and Susan Bernofsky (Columbia, 2013). Jean Boase-Beier's *Translating the Poetry of the Holocaust: Translation, Style and the Reader* (Bloomsbury, 2015) was an informative academic work. I also found great if bracing inspiration about the art of translation in Eliot Weinberger's *19 Ways of Looking at Wang Wei* (New Directions, 1987; 2016) and Robyn Creswell's interview with Michael Hofmann in *The Paris Review*, no. 230 (Fall 2019).

NOTES TO THE POEMS

Sachs is not only an intertextual poet, whose oeuvre, poem by poem, establishes its own symbolic network across individual volumes, but also an intratextual one, continually allusive, drawing from works of Kabbalah, such as the *Zohar*, as well as the Bible, and Christian mystics such as Jakob Böhme, Meister Eckhart, and Simone Weil. *Flight and Metamorphosis* contains echoes of and references to a cosmogony that is, like Kabbalah—the work she was most in touch with at the time—a fusion of influences, an integration of elements that never reveals any referential key to Sachs's work, as if it were written in a symbolical code that exists outside the world the poems create.

The conceits and objects of Kabbalah are thus only one source Sachs draws from in the invention of her own language; it would render the poems overdetermined to provide notes that indicate otherwise. What follow, then, are meant to be suggestive connections only, drawn from some of the works she had read or was reading at the time of composition, and other information that might be pertinent to a particular poem. I also provide some references that might escape a reader such as myself, ones I would be thankful to have in hand. Obvious references such as Bible characters, and other subjects easily looked up, I leave to the reader. There is much that remains beyond the scope of what can be managed in a modest apparatus. The aim of this translation is to showcase the poetry first and foremost (which is what I go to poetry for—the poetry), and to provide some of the context for understanding what it is and where it came from.

Notes for one poem can often be applied to others; one function of the notes is to suggest Sachs's allusive web of shadings, inflections, and echoes.

SOURCES CITED IN THE NOTES

Martin Buber, *I and Thou*, trans. Ronald Gregor Smith (1923; Scribner's, 1958).

———, *The Legend of the Baal-Shem*, trans. Maurice Friedman (1955; Princeton, 1995).

Peter Cole, *The Poetry of Kabbalah* (Yale, 2012).

Aris Fioretos, *Nelly Sachs, Flight and Metamorphosis*, trans. Tomas Tranæus (Suhrkamp, 2010; Stanford, 2011).

James L. Kugel, *Traditions of the Bible* (Harvard, 1998).

Nelly Sachs, *Briefe*, eds. Ruth Dinesen and Helmut Müssener (Suhrkamp, 1984).

Gershom Scholem, *Major Trends in Jewish Mysticism* (Schocken, 1946; 1954).

———, ed., *Zohar, the Book of Splendor* (Schocken, 1949; 1977).

———, *On the Kabbalah and Its Symbolism*, trans. Ralph Manheim (Schocken, 1960; 1965).

Simone Weil, *Gravity and Grace*, trans. Emma Crawford and Mario von der Ruhr (1947; Routledge, 1952).

NOTES

Who dies / here last

grain of sun—"The kingdom of heaven is like a grain of mustard seed." Weil (1947): 111.

"The first ray of divine light is also the primeval germ of creation." Scholem (1946): 227.

tomb—The German word, *Gottesacker*, translates literally as *God's acre*, the proverbial figure for the burial ground of a churchyard. My choice of *tomb* is an interpolation.

This is the dark breath

sacred writing—"[God] drew them [the 22 letters of the Hebrew alphabet], hewed them, combined them, weighed them, interchanged them, and through them produced the whole creation and everything that is destined to be created." Scholem quotes from *Sefer Yetsirah* or Book of Creation (in *Maaseh Beresith*). Each letter, he explains, has a secret meaning in the "three realms of creation [...] man, the world of the stars and planets, and the rhythmic flow of time." Scholem (1946): 76.

"[The] concordance between letters as the elements of the world of language and atoms as the elements of reality was already noted by certain of the Greek philosophers [...] [e.g.,] Democritus' idea [...] which recurs in Kabbalistic theory of the Torah; namely, that the same letters in different combinations reproduce the different aspects of the world." Scholem (1960): 77.

"As the Kabbalists saw them, angels were emanations of the divine light that does God's work in the world. Others have seen them as thoughts, or even as letters." Cole (2012): 361.

Laocoön—the Trojan priest set upon by god-sent serpents. The famous Hellenistic sculpture *Laocoön and His Sons* (on display at the Vatican) is central to Gotthold Ephraim Lessing's *Laocoön: An Essay on the Limits of Painting and Poetry* (1766). Sachs, on her mother's side, was related to Lessing and lived for a while on Lessingstrasse in Berlin. Fioretos (2010): 146.

sprouting in our pupil—"But from somewhere a seed fell into his sleep, and a dream sprouted and grew." Buber (1955): 158.

rushing shell of secrets—"the closed shell of [God's] hidden self." Scholem (1946): 209. The German word, *Geheimnisse*, translates as *secrets*, or *mysteries*; it carries both meanings. I have opted to translate *Geheimnisse* as mystery more often, as that corresponds more immediately than *secrets* to both the Jewish (kabbalistic) and the Christian mystery of God's hidden presence in the world.

How light / the earth will be

like a nightmare / on the human breast—See Henry Fuseli's painting *The Nightmare* (1781). Detroit Institute of Arts.

"The *Zohar* speaks expressly of such a nothing, it is always taken as God's innermost mode of being, which becomes creative in the emanation of the *sefiroth* [the potencies and modes of action of the living God]. 'Nothing' is itself the first and highest of the *sefiroth*. It is the 'root of all roots,' from which the tree draws nourishment." Scholem (1960): 103.

The Hunter

The Hunter—Orion, from Greek mythology, and one of the most prominent of the constellations, easily seen all over the world.

rest on the flight—"Rest on the flight into Egypt" is a topos in the Western tradition of art of the Holy Family (Joseph, Mary, and the infant Jesus) fleeing Roman persecution.

So far out, in the open

nightdress body / stretching its emptiness—"Of late my soul has been departing from me in the night" [from *Zohar*]. Scholem (1949): 27.

"According to Jewish tradition, the soul [...] leaves the body each night while we sleep; it returns each dawn with God's kiss, which wakes us and seals the bond of body and soul for another day." Cole (2012): 173.

Sacred minute / filled with departing

the most beloved—Sachs often described her mother as her "most beloved." Fioretos (2010): 26. The figure of "the beloved" can also refer in Sachs's work to her one great lost love (with whom she never consummated her affections), killed by the Nazis. (His name remains unknown.)

Ram, Pisces, Lion—the constellations.

when the soul's not home—According to Jewish legend, as discussed in the
previous note, the soul is not at home in the body when it sleeps. If the
soul never returns from its astral travel, the body dies; the soul wanders
forever.

In flight

feet in the sand's prayer—n.b. In the Bible, sand is a recurring metaphor
for the children of Israel.

from fin to wing—In biblical midrash, Moses requests that God transform
him into a bird so that he might reach the promised land. Kugel (1998):
885.

The sick butterfly—After her mother's death in 1950, Sachs refers to her as
"this veined butterfly soul, now so full of the dark pain of the world, and
which had long prepared for departure and anxiously beat her wings."
Fioretos (2010): 138.

"The It [things of the world] is the eternal chrysalis, the Thou the eternal
butterfly." A figure of transformative process in man's relation to the di-
vine. Buber (1923): 17.

This stone / with the fly's inscription / has dropped into my hand—Stones
are tokens of God's compassion. It's said that living stones fell from
heaven, connecting heaven to earth. In other Semitic legends, humans
are born of stone.

Dancer

Dancer / like a bride—"Already as a child my greatest wish was to become
a dancer [. . .] Dance became my form of expression even before words
did. My innermost element." Letter to Walter Berendsohn, 1.25.59, Fiore-
tos (2010): 49.

The Shekinah, the female principle of God's "indwelling" creative power on
earth, is often figured in Kabbalah as a bride, living in exile in her search
for the divine, figured as a groom. The wedding, for Hasidim, enacts this

symbolic unification, God's "oneness," in the formal reuniting of God's female and male nature (the female manifest on earth, the male hidden). The *mitzvah tanz*, or wedding dance, is a celebration of this joining.

Dancer / twisting in labor—"I believe in the working through of pain, in the dust's consummate animations as a labor in which we are a part. I believe in an invisible universe, into which we write our unclear fulfillment." Letter to Margit Abenius 12.30.57. Fioretos (2010): 202.

"At times [the ecstasy of high holiness] expresses itself in an action, consecrates it and fills it with holy meaning. The purest form—that in which the whole body serves the aroused soul and in which each of the soul's risings and bendings creates a visible symbol corresponding to it, allowing one image of enraptured meaning to emerge out of a thousand waves of movement—is the dance." Buber (1955): 21.

Just look

a straight candle—"It can be said that he who cares to pierce into the mystery of the holy unity of God should consider the flame as it rises from a burning coal or candle" [from Zohar]. Scholem (1949): 14.

David / chosen

of the most solitary hour / became an eye / and saw—"But is not solitude, too, a gate? Is there not at times disclosed, in stillest loneliness, an unsuspected perception? Can concern with oneself not mysteriously be transformed into concern with the mystery?" Buber (1923): 103.

For a long time / Jacob

Jacob / with the blessing of his arm—See Rembrandt's painting *Jacob Blessing the Sons of Joseph* (1656). Schloss Wilhelmshöhe, Kassel.

the flash of false blessing—With his right hand, Jacob blesses the younger son, rather than the elder (as was custom). Rembrandt's painting depicts Joseph's fruitless attempt to "deflect" or correct the position of Jacob's hands.

Hallelujah

For the epigraph, see Job 5:23.
Sealed-up star-garments—"And those days in which he did righteously and sinned not become for his soul a garment of splendor" [from *Zohar*]. Scholem (1949): 40.
in the sapphire-blossom that breathes the medusa—the medusa, a jellyfish.

Already / crackling, colored

the compass rose—the figure on a compass showing the cardinal directions; also called a windrose.

This century / springs

Berenice's Hair—the constellation (Coma Berenices) in the northern sky named after Queen Berenice II of Egypt, who gave up her hair as an offering to Aphrodite.

With no compass

the cup of trembling in the sea—Isaiah 51:22.
of the great mother—"the mythical saying of the Jews, 'in the mother's body man knows the universe, in birth he forgets it' [. . .] Every child that is coming into being rests, like all life that is coming into being, in the womb of the great mother, the undivided primal world that precedes form. From her, too, we are separated, and enter into personal life, slipping free only in the dark hours to be close to her again." Buber (1923): 25.

Yet where in the mists

Yet where in the mists / shall we seek the roots of those breaths—"En-Sof [. . .] the hidden Root of all Roots [. . .] the hidden God." Scholem (1946): 214.

White serpent

flaming shell of fury—In German, *Granate* can mean *shell, bomb,* or *grenade*; but it is also associated by root with *pomegranate,* or *Granatapfel,* a reference to the shape of the fruit.

How many homelands

n.b. In all editions, the first strophe of this poem does not end with a period or other form of punctuation; however, the parallelism of phrasing between first and second strophe reinforces the feeling of one. Nonetheless, the translation follows the original.

Deep inside / the station of suffering

Stella Maris, lodestar of certainty—literally, Star of the Sea. Polaris; the North Star. Also, a late medieval title for the Virgin Mary.

Behind the lips

the wailing wall—The German word, *Klagemauer,* translates literally as *wailing wall*. The Western Wall, in the southwest of the old city of Jerusalem, known as "the wailing wall," is the last remnant of the Jewish Temple, the most important Jewish sanctuary, which was destroyed by the Romans in AD 70.

ACKNOWLEDGMENTS

I am indebted to Linda Parshall for her exacting expertise, deep knowledge, wide learning, honed intuition, hours of dedication, comradery, friendship, generosity, and spirited willingness to step into the unknown.

XL thanks to Jonathan Galassi for his unwavering support and encouragement, his expertise, and also his patience. The manuscript improved with his eye on it. To Hans Magnus Enzensberger and the editors at Suhrkamp Verlag for permission and some faith, my gratitude. I thank Susan Brown for her fine attention to the copyedit, and Katharine Liptak for shepherding the script, and me, through the proper gates. The intuitive and stunning book design by Crisis deserves a warm embrace—thank you!

A deep bow to readers of the translation in various stages, who listened carefully to my efforts and made corrections and suggestions with encouraging good humor and sympathy: Don Berger, Alexander Booth, Katharina Erben, Robert Felfe, Susanne Gerber, Regina Hanneman, Ellen Hinsey, Nikola Irmer, Alistair Noon, Peter Schmidt, Tom Sleigh, Donna Stonecipher, Uljana Wolf, Mark Wunderlich. David Gewanter, Jonathan Rosen, and Linda Voris were helpful readers of the introduction. Peter Parshall helped identify some (to me) obscure ekphrastic passages without breaking a sweat on his way to and from the espresso machine. About Kabbalah, and other aspects of Judaism, I learned more than I could handle (as usual) from my aunt Rabbi Cheryl Weiner, who also read the introduction with care.

The Department of English and the Graduate School at University of Maryland provided time and material support, including a 2019 Creative and Performing Arts Award, crucial to the completion of the book.

This project started with a John Simon Guggenheim Memorial Foundation fellowship and a grant from the Institute for the International Education of Students Abroad program in Berlin, both of which provided material support for the research and writing of *Berlin Notebook: Where Are the Refugees?*, published by *Los Angeles Review of Books* as a digital edition in 2016. That work, in turn, led me to Nelly Sachs—or I should say, led me back round to her, in Schöneberg, my *Bezirk* in Berlin, and the district, too, of Alexander Booth, who physically put Sachs's *The Seeker* in my hands and egged me on with the sympathetic smile of an expert translator. He knew what I was getting into long before I did, and he never let on. Still (!), a second thanks.

And thanks to Don Share at *Poetry*, Carolyn Kuebler and Rick Barot at *New England Review*, Julia Leverone at *AzonaL*, and Bill Carty at *Poetry Northwest* for publishing some of the poems along the way, some in slightly different versions. Some of these poems were republished online at *Literary Hub* and *Poetry Daily*.

For the finest company along the way, essential sustenance, boundless support, and love beyond measure, my thanks and gratitude to Sarah Blake, for the freedom of a shared life. For Eli and Gus, these ancient roots for new branching.